Exiting Prostitution

Exiting Prostitution

A Study in Female Desistance

Roger Matthews
Professor of Criminology, University of Kent, UK

Helen Easton
Senior Lecturer, London South Bank University, UK

Lisa Young
Research and Development Officer, Eaves, UK

Julie Bindel
Journalist and Researcher, UK

First published 2014 by
PALGRAVE MACMILLAN

Palgrave Macmillan in the UK is an imprint of Macmillan Publishers Limited, registered in England, company number 785998, of Houndmills, Basingstoke, Hampshire RG21 6XS.

Palgrave Macmillan in the US is a division of St Martin's Press LLC, 175 Fifth Avenue, New York, NY 10010.

Palgrave Macmillan is the global academic imprint of the above companies and has companies and representatives throughout the world.

Palgrave® and Macmillan® are registered trademarks in the United States, the United Kingdom, Europe and other countries.

ISBN 978–1–137–28941–4 hardback
ISBN 978–1–137–28940–7 paperback

This book is printed on paper suitable for recycling and made from fully managed and sustained forest sources. Logging, pulping and manufacturing processes are expected to conform to the environmental regulations of the country of origin.

A catalogue record for this book is available from the British Library.

Library of Congress Cataloging-in-Publication Data
Matthews, Roger, 1948–
   Exiting prostitution : a study in female desistance / Roger Matthews, Helen Easton, Lisa Young, Julie Bindel.
      pages   cm
   ISBN 978–1–137–28941–4 (hardback) —
   ISBN 978–1–137–28940–7 (paperback)
   1. Prostitution—Great Britain.   2. Prostitutes—Rehabilitation—Great Britain.   I. Title.
HQ185.A5M37 2014
306.740941—dc23   2014025007

Contents

Figures

Preface

This book draws mainly on the PEER research project funded by the National Lottery, and was carried out by Eaves (http://www.eavesforwomen.org.uk) and London South Bank University between 2010 and 2012. The research took a multi-method approach, drawing on both quantitative and qualitative methods. These included contact with women involved in or exiting prostitution or formerly trafficked women as well as interviews with practitioners and other relevant professionals. Fieldwork was conducted in seven locations across England, with women participating in the study in Doncaster, Ipswich, Leeds, London, Newcastle, Southampton and Sheffield. The research incorporated visual methods and the use of personal journals by participants. Interviews collected information about women's current and personal circumstances as well as an in-depth life history interview and visual mapping exercise.

Some 114 women (55 of whom had exited prostitution) participated in the face-to-face interviews. Of these, 73 were or had been involved in street prostitution, 6 in brothels, 13 in private premises and 12 as escorts. We also interviewed 7 women who had been trafficked. Three women sold sex in clubs. In all, 117 interviews were undertaken, but 3 were not completed; the total number of completed interviews with women was therefore 114. A total of 35 semi-structured interviews were undertaken with stakeholders across 10 sites in England and Wales.

Ethical approval for the research was obtained from both the London South Bank University Research Ethics Committee and the Central London (Camden and Islington) NHS Research Ethics Committee. A research advisory group was convened to provide external guidance for the research and as a regular point of consultation in relation to research tool design, ethical issues and as a testing ground for preliminary findings. The group consisted of ten members including specialist practitioners, academics, members of the Metropolitan Police Service and local government policymakers.

Acknowledgements

The authors would like to thank the following people for assisting with this book: Denise Marshall, Ruth Breslin, Heather Harvey and Laura Brown at Eaves, as well as the helpful comments and suggestions on earlier drafts of the book by Professor Shadd Maruna and Helen Johnson.

We would also like to thank all the members of the advisory group for the PEER project, including Ann Hamilton, Catherine Allen, Di Martin, Dr. Georgina Smith, Jaqui Hunt, Professor Jalna Hanmer, Maggie Warwick, Professor Margaret Melrose and Detective Inspector Steve Wilkinson. The members of the advisory group provided valuable advice and guidance on the research.

Thanks also go to all the stakeholders who agreed to be interviewed and shared their experiences, as well as to all the women who participated in the research and who gave up their time to express their views on their involvement in prostitution and their experience of exiting.

Finally, thanks go to the Big Lottery Fund for its generous support.

1
The Dynamics of Exiting and Desistance

Introduction

There has been a considerable amount written about women's entry into prostitution but relatively little about how they exit. Over the past decade, however, there has been growing interest in the exiting process. This interest has been stimulated on one hand by a steady stream of sociological and criminological literature on desistance and on the other by the growing realisation that a large percentage of women involved in prostitution would like to exit if they could (Audet and Carrier 2006; Bradford 2005; Farley 2004; Hough and Rice 2008; Ng and Venticich 2006; O'Neill and Campbell 2011).

It has been found in various studies that few women see prostitution as a long-term 'career' but that most aim to be involved for a limited period of time, either to deal with financial or personal issues, or to finance drug habits. Some women take breaks from prostitution to take up 'formal' employment for certain periods and return to prostitution at a later date (Melrose et al. 1999). Significantly, a recent review of trends in Glasgow found that in the late 1990s that there were an estimated 1,100 women involved in street prostitution and that by 2010 the number had decreased to approximately 250 (Matthews and Easton 2011; McKeganey 2005). This dramatic decrease serves as a salient reminder that women do leave prostitution over time in considerable numbers, and that in some cases they leave with a minimal amount of formal intervention.

In contrast, the successful removal of prostitution from the streets of Ipswich following the murders of five women in December 2006

involved the implementation of a coordinated multi-agency intervention (Poland et al. 2008). The key to this success was, on one
hand, the provision of an integrated and comprehensive set of services that linked exiting to prevention work, while tackling demand;
and on the other, the adoption of a multi-agency case conference
approach for each of the women involved in street prostitution.
This type of individualised case management approach has also been
adopted to some extent in Manchester, Leeds and Glasgow. The
aim is to develop a care plan and personalised programme that can
engage with the women on a one-to-one basis and facilitate exiting.
What is also significant about the exiting programmes that have been
developed in these locations is that they all challenge the view that
prostitution is here to stay and believe that a substantial reduction
in the level of prostitution is not only desirable but also possible
(Lawrence 2007; Manchester Prostitution Strategy 2007; Matthews
and Easton 2011; Scottish Executive 2004; Ward 2007).

Explaining desistance

Desistance is usually defined as the end of a period of involvement in
addictive or deviant behaviour. However, it is always possible that
those who have overcome addictions or stopped offending for a
period may return at a later date. Consequently, it is always uncertain
whether individuals have actually desisted or just stopped engaging
in an activity for the period under consideration (Maruna 2001).
Thus, although there is always a degree of arbitrariness involved in
defining forms of desistance, for our purposes 'stopping' is defined
as ceasing involvement in prostitution for up to three months, while
'exiting' refers to those women who have ceased their involvement in
prostitution for at least three months. Normally, the process of exiting is seen to involve the construction of a post-prostitution identity
and the adoption of an ex-role.

For the most part, studies to date have operated with a zero-sum
conception of exiting. That is, an assessment is made of whether
women are still involved in prostitution or whether they have ceased
involvement altogether. However, many women will for one reason
or another reduce their involvement in prostitution over time. It is
important to find out, however, whether this reduction is linked
to efforts to exit or not. By the same token, developing strategies

to facilitate exiting based solely on the final state of termination is unlikely to fully illuminate this complex process (Kanzemain 2007).

The growing focus on desistance has drawn attention to the issue of how people make radical changes in lifestyle over time and how they overcome various forms of addiction or cease their involvement in certain forms of behaviour. Among the most influential contributors to the literature on desistance has been the work of Sampson and Laub (1993). Adopting a form of longitudinal analysis, they have sought to identify the main factors that underpin significant changes in the life-course and suggest that gaining employment or entering a marriage or other stable relationship are amongst the most significant events that can affect desistance. Importantly, they argue that many of the classic predictors of onset and frequency of offending do not explain desistance. They also note that groups such as drug users do not follow the usual 'routes out'. Desistance, they suggest, is a process rather than an event and it is subject to reversals and failure. However, the causal relationship between desistance and employment and marriage has been questioned, and while it may be the case that these events are the most important factors for some groups, they may not be for certain marginalised groups, such as women involved in prostitution (Vaughan 2007).

Gender and desistance

It is evident that even amongst the limited literature on desistance the vast majority is directed towards men, particularly young men. The research that has looked at women has shown both similarities and differences in the nature of desistance for men and women. Graham and Bowling (1995), for example, found that becoming an adult (e.g. leaving home, finishing schooling or starting a family) was related to desistance for women, but the same was not true for men. Sommers et al. (1994) on the other hand found that the factors associated with female desistance from street crime were very similar to those reported in male street offenders.

Giordano et al. (2002) found that neither marital attachment nor job stability was strongly related to female desistance, although they note that the cognitive transformations made by men and women tended to be similar and that maturation was a key factor in the desistance process for both groups. McIvor et al. (2004) found that while men explained their desistance in utilitarian terms, women often alluded to the moral dimensions of their activities. Thus, it is suggested that women's desistance has a more pronounced 'relational' dimension. Interestingly, McIvor et al. (2004) and her colleagues note that many of the women in their study were keen to be viewed as desisting, even if they continued to offend. Also, the authors emphasise that it is important to distinguish between attitudinal and behavioural change when thinking about desistance. Relatedly, it is suggested by Graham and Bowling (1995) that disengaging from delinquent peers, whether consciously or by chance, is a necessary condition for desistance for some women.

The focus on gender difference suggests that if the process of desistance is different for men and women there may also be differences in relation to race and class (Katz 2000; O'Neill and Campbell 2011). In a similar way, given that women involved in prostitution are not a homogenous group, there may be significant differences amongst women involved in different forms of prostitution. Sanders (2007) has raised the question of whether exiting is different for street-based women and those who work indoors. It is also the case that 'exiting' has a very different meaning for trafficked women, given the role of coercion and deception in relation to their involvement in prostitution (Anti-Trafficking Monitoring Group 2010).

Barriers to exiting

Although studies repeatedly indicate that a large proportion of women involved in prostitution would like to exit, there are a number of formidable obstacles that women have to confront and overcome if they plan to leave prostitution. For many commentators, dealing with drug addiction is identified as a major issue, since it is estimated that in the UK some 70–90 per cent of women who work on the streets are problematic drug users (May and Hunter 2006). In most cases the drugs of choice are heroin and crack cocaine, the latter being particularly addictive and personally and socially destructive (Bourgois 2003; Goldstein 1979).

The question has been raised, however, of the extent to which drug use and addiction precedes, or is exacerbated, by involvement in prostitution (Potterat et al. 1998). It has also been suggested that the links between drug use, prostitution and other forms of social exclusion may be overplayed (Buchanan 2004; Melrose 2007). Problematic drug use, however, is frequently found to be linked to other vulnerabilities and needs, while homelessness has been identified as a recurring issue amongst women involved in prostitution and many women report financial and health problems that can act as a barrier to exiting (Benoit and Millar 2001; Pitcher 2006).

Apart from these widely recognised obstacles, women involved in prostitution tend to refer to problems of lifestyle, boredom and above all money (Hoigard and Finstad 1992). Relatedly, women involved in prostitution tend to have low levels of skills, poor employment histories and limited social capital. Consequently, the employment opportunities that are available are often low paid menial or temporary jobs (Hough and Rice 2008). In some cases the main barrier to exiting is the pressure from coercive and abusive partners/pimps, a proportion of whom are themselves problematic drug users (Poland et al. 2008; Ward 2007). The problem of dealing with coercive and abusive partners has moved agencies in some areas to see this as a domestic violence issue and has fostered attempts to treat women involved in prostitution and their partners simultaneously (Boynton 1998; Rice 2010). According to Hoigard and Finstad (1992), underpinning these various obstacles are problems of shame, issues of identity, a sense of insecurity and the difficulties in overcoming marginalisation and stigmatisation.

Another barrier to exiting that has been identified by a number of researchers and activists in different countries is women's involvement in the criminal justice system (Hubbard 2006; Pitcher 2006). Involvement in the criminal justice system for prostitution-related offences is seen to increase women's vulnerability on one hand, and to make it difficult for them to gain legitimate employment, on the other. Thus there is a growing body of opinion amongst those who are trying to develop exiting programmes that soliciting for the purposes of prostitution should be decriminalised (PAAFE 2005).

What works and best practice

The interest in exiting in the UK was increased significantly by the publication of *Tackling Street Prostitution: A Holistic Approach* by Hester and Westmarland (2004) and the subsequent official endorsement of exiting programmes in the Home Office publication *A Co-ordinated Prostitution Strategy* (Home Office 2006). Hester and Westmarland (2004) have provided an evaluation of a number of exiting projects that have been established in England and Wales. In their examination, they concluded that provision needs to be holistic and integrated in order to meet the complex needs of women seeking support. They suggested that outreach is a significant prerequisite for building a sustainable working relationship with the women, while providing one-to-one support. They emphasised the need for fast-track drugs programmes and the provision of emergency accommodation where possible. Although Hester and Westmarland (2004) sought to identify 'what works' in relation to the exiting projects that they examined, they note that measuring change presented difficulties and that much of the exiting provision was 'crisis driven'. Consequently, they found it difficult to attribute change to specific interventions. They note that because different projects operated with different philosophies, policies and practices and used different definitions of 'engagement' and 'exiting', it was difficult if not impossible to determine 'what works' with any degree of confidence.

Other evaluations of exiting projects have encountered similar problems. The evaluation of Project Respect's Pathways Project, based in Melbourne, Australia, for example, identifies 'success' in terms of the number of women attending particular programmes together with statements from service users regarding the perceived benefits (Lewis and Montague 2008). However, there is little in this form of evaluation about 'what works' in terms of desistance or of assessing the effect of different interventions on the process of change (Christian et al. 2009). The evaluation of the Safe Exit Diversion Scheme in London, which is principally a scheme designed to divert women from the criminal justice system, found that it helped women to build more stable lives and increase their engagement with services. However, the number of women exiting prostitution in the review period was minimal and it is not clear what worked for them (Rice 2010). The author of the report also notes that while the provision of emergency accommodation is seen as a positive response to homelessness and associated vulnerability, it was reported that living in hostels with other vulnerable, marginalised and drug-dependent women can in some cases make it hard to give up prostitution and drug use.

Drawing on the work of Hester and Westmarland (2004), Mayhew and Mossman (2007) attempt to move beyond what they see as an unduly narrow focus on 'what works' and instead to aim to identify examples of 'good practice' in relation to exiting. They point out that while there are useful qualitative and quantitative components in some of the evaluations of exiting programmes, most are based on small samples and fail to identify the impact of specific interventions. Instead, Mayhew and Mossman (2007) want to examine the design and implementation of initiatives in order to determine the best practice principles for exiting. However, since exiting strategies often form part of a package, Mayhew and Mossman face the same difficulties as the 'what works' approach, as it is difficult to differentiate best practice examples for exiting interventions from the spectrum of general support services for women involved in prostitution. However, they summarise what they see as the best practice principles for exiting prostitution. These include:

- The provision of holistic interventions
- Facilitating choice and flexibility
- Providing a dedicated service
- Building trusting relationships
- Developing good communication to enlisting public support for exiting programmes
- Developing outreach services
- Developing local, user-friendly services for women.

Developing a 'holistic' approach?

One point of agreement between Hester and Westmarland (2004) and Mayhew and Mossman (2007) is an emphasis on the adoption of a 'holistic' approach, which is seen as necessary to provide an effective response to the complex needs of women involved in prostitution. Thus Hester and Westmarland (2004) strongly suggest that:

> Holistic support, which includes a range of mechanisms of support services (outreach to engage those involved in prostitution, one-to-one work and fast track drug services), geared to the individual needs of women involved in prostitution, are more likely to result

in exit from prostitution. This should be central to any approach tackling street prostitution.

(Hester and Westmarland 2004: 40)

The call for the adoption of a holistic approach has been extremely influential in the literature on exiting and a considerable number of commentators have echoed this sentiment. However, there is some uncertainty about what constitutes a holistic approach, how such an approach should be applied and what combination of policies and practices defines an approach as 'holistic' (Clark and Squires 2005; Colley 2003; Harcourt et al. 2005; Saphira and Oliver 2002).

The dictionary defines 'holism' as 'the treatment of any subject as a totally integrated system' and states that it involves 'treating the whole person rather than just symptoms of a disease'. Holistic approaches are widely seen as preferable to those approaches that provide a partial, selective or an uncoordinated response. On one level, it is difficult to argue against the adoption of a holistic approach and it is widely viewed as preferable to piecemeal forms of intervention. However, the question arises about what needs are relevant to the process of exiting and how those needs are to be identified and dealt with. Clearly, all the person's needs cannot be dealt with, and the difficulty is identifying relevant needs and prioritising certain needs over others. Often this is linked to conceptions of risk.

Our task, therefore, should not be to try to identify all the person's needs but rather to develop a tailored and strategic approach that aims to identify those needs or risks that are associated with exiting. In this way the identification and response to needs is necessarily selective and targeted. However, identifying the needs that require attention in order to exit is far from obvious. It is not the objective of intervention to deal with the 'whole person' and to work on the assumption that *all* the person's needs have to be addressed before they are able to exit. Thus in practice the required response provided is always likely to be less than 'holistic'. Needs that are not linked to exiting can be dealt with, if necessary, after the person has left prostitution. Thus it would seem that there are three limitations to the practical adoption of a 'holistic' needs-based strategy. The first is deciding what constitutes relevant needs. The second is deciding which issues need addressing in what order if the aim is to help women leave prostitution. Third, the focus on individual attributes all too often tends to be divorced from wider social contexts.

The corollary of trying to develop a 'holistic' or integrated approach is the development of a coordinated multi-agency approach, in order to address the person's multiple vulnerabilities. Again, at first sight this appears very positive and desirable. However, research has repeatedly shown the limitations of multi-agency approaches and the recurring problems of coordination (Crawford 1998). It is the case that each agency tends to have its own priorities, view of the issues, and set of practices and principles. This is likely to involve differences in perception, diagnosis and response. In effect, the different agencies rarely respond to the person as a whole but rather deal with particular issues. This leads to what Haggarty and Ericson (2000) refer to as the 'surveillant assemblage', which 'separates human bodies from their territorial settings, while separating them into a series of discrete flows'. Moreover, since the identification of (relevant) needs is uncertain, it is not always clear which agencies are required and how they might be effectively coordinated. In some cases the appropriate services may not provide the type of services requested, often resulting in the adoption of a more piecemeal and selective approach than the notion of 'holistic' would suggest.

All too often support agencies concentrate on the vulnerabilities and problems that women face. This approach can be characterised as a 'deficit model'. From this vantage point exiting is to be achieved by removing these 'deficits'. It is paradoxical that many support agencies and researchers that claim they want to 'empower' women involved in prostitution all too often present them as little more than a bundle of unresolved needs. However, rather than adopt this largely negative deficit model, which aims to promote exiting by overcoming unmet needs and vulnerabilities, it might be more productive to simply ask the women concerned what they require in order to exit prostitution. This may involve not only focusing on their unmet needs but also on the more positive aspects of their lives. That is, rather than concentrate on their shortcomings it may be more appropriate to place more emphasis on a 'strengths' and 'opportunities' model that explores women's interests, aspirations and capacity for change. The focus on strengths may well provide women with a positive view of their capabilities and abilities, which in turn may help them to deal with their various vulnerabilities.

Ward and his colleagues have developed a 'strengths-based' approach which they call 'The Good Lives Model' (Ward and Brown 2004; Ward and Maruna 2007). Based on the assumption that most people given the opportunity want fulfilling lives, it suggests that intervention should speak directly to women's self-interest. The Good Lives Model aims to focus on positive change, personal development and the achievement of identified goals. Rather than using only the language of deficiency and inadequacy, it aims to construct a positive approach linked to the development of skills and competencies in order to try to achieve a more satisfying life. Practically, this means that more attention should be paid to the identification of the person's aspirations and aims, while working together to identify how these objectives might be realised. Developing an approach that is able to incorporate both the person's vulnerabilities and their attributes might more properly be referred to as 'holistic'.

Stages of change

In most of the exiting projects that are considered to be examples of 'good practice', a recurring feature is the provision of a staged approach to exiting. Although these projects tend to operate with slightly different stages, they all tend to incorporate a developmental approach that is used to gauge the points of transition from involvement in prostitution to exiting or stopping (Prochaska et al. 1992; Ebaugh 1988; Levesque et al. 1999). The advantage of developing a staged model of exiting, it is suggested, is that it allows the monitoring of the development or progression of service users. Such a model is based on the assumption that exiting is rarely an event and more a process. A staged model is seen to provide service users with a framework and set of objectives to which they can aspire. It is also claimed that operating such a model makes it easier to monitor and evaluate progress and achievement, while making it possible to tailor treatment programmes that fit with the situations and development of different women.

Probably the best-known model of the stages of change is that presented by Prochaska et al. (1992), which is based on psychotherapy. They have developed a five-stage model which is seen to apply to all forms of addictive behaviour. The five stages of change that have been identified are: (1) *precontemplation*, the stage at which there is no intention to change behaviour in the foreseeable future;

(2) *contemplation*, the stage at which people are aware that a problem exists and are seriously thinking about overcoming it but have not made a commitment to take action; (3) *preparation*, the stage at which people begin to think about taking action in the near future; (4) *action*, the stage at which individuals modify their behaviour, experiences or environment in order to overcome their problems; and (5) *maintenance*, the stage at which people work to prevent relapse and consolidate the gains attained during the action stage.

Critics of the stage model argue that this approach oversimplifies the complexities of behavioural change by imposing artificial categories on a continuous process. Littell and Girvin (2002), for example, in a detailed review of the trans-theoretical model of change presented by Prochaska and her colleagues, conclude that: 'there is little empirical evidence of sequential transitions between stages and that the model lacks predictive power about who is likely to complete all stages'. The trans-theoretical model is also criticised for not paying attention to external factors and for not differentiating between problem types (Farrall and Bowling 1999).

Littell and Girvin argue that the underlying notion of the rational actor on which the stages model is based is flawed. At the same time they argue that different groups of people involved in different types of activities will experience change in different ways, and that the model is too rigid on one hand and too narrow on the other. They suggest that:

> Successful change processes may vary depending on the nature and the complexity of the target behavior, presence of other problems, external stressors and supports and cultural context. The search for a generic, underlying structure of behavioral change has led to unnecessary reductionism, reliance on a set of categories that do not reflect qualitatively different states, and adherence to assumptions about stage progression that have not been supported. The model cannot have practical utility for the design or allocation of treatment services if its basic tenets do not hold up. It is time to seriously consider alternative conceptualizations of change processes.
>
> (Littell and Girvin 2002: 253)

This critique resonates with our own findings. Although we began our study by trying to adapt a stages approach to this group of women, it soon became apparent that it was a poor fit. Most of the women were found to occupy a number of stages simultaneously, and their exiting pathways were rarely found to follow this type of sequential path. Women were working on changing identities at the same time as they were undergoing treatment, while in other cases exiting was trigged by external events to which the women responded. We also found that in some cases women exited prostitution fairly spontaneously rather than moving through discernible 'stages' while others simply skipped 'stages'. It became evident in the course of the research that the 'stages' presented by Prochaska and others were not so much a description of the process of change but an 'ideal type' of how researchers have come to depict the process. Thus the stages model is prescriptive rather than descriptive and suggests how people should change or how they might be encouraged to change.

Other sequential accounts put forward by Ebaugh (1988), Mansson and Hedin (1999) and Herman (1992) suffer from similar problems. Ebaugh (1988), for example, has presented a 'role exit' model that involves four main stages: (1) first doubts, (2) alternatives, (3) turning points and (4) creating an exit role. The aim, Ebaugh argues, is to encourage desisters to distance themselves from their old role and try to establish a new one. However, it has been argued with some justification that Ebaugh's approach lacks a theory of action and is therefore unable to understand the process by which people develop new roles (Wacquant 1990).

Baker et al. (2010) drawing on the research carried out by Dalla (2006) argue that there is empirical support for both the stages of change model developed by Prochaska et al. (1992) and the role of exit model presented by Ebaugh (1988). The authors argue, however, that the model presented by Prochaska and her colleagues is too general and does not address the specificity or complexity of the obstacles facing women who want to leave prostitution. Both approaches also fail, they suggest, by not allowing for the social isolation and stigmatisation that can affect women involved in prostitution, while at the same time not clearly distinguishing between the impact of formal and informal support systems. In contrast to the previous models, Baker et al. (2010) present what they see as an integrated model involving six stages. Unfortunately, the model that they develop does not overcome the various limitations of the other models of change, but rather compounds them.

Mansson and Hedin (1999) have made a useful contribution to this issue by focusing on the interaction between internal and external factors. Drawing on the work of Sampson and Laub (1993) as well as Ebaugh (1988), Mansson and Hedin focus on 'turning points' defined as 'eye-opening' events, or traumatic events such as violent experiences, or positive life experiences such as finding a new partner as catalysts of desistance. These 'turning points' may be sudden, but in most cases are medium and long term processes that serve to reduce involvement in prostitution. For Mansson and Hedin the exiting process normally involves a combination of structural, relational and individual factors. Thus, apart from having alternative employment opportunities or the necessary motivation, emphasis is placed on the importance of relational processes in facilitating exiting. They emphasise that a critical element of the exiting process is women's ability to mobilise both informal and professional support. This support is seen as necessary in many cases to help work through traumatic experiences and build new social networks (Hedin and Mansson 2003). According to Hedin and Mansson, after the 'breakaway' women struggle with four main issues: working through and understanding the experience of life in prostitution, dealing with shame, living in a marginal situation, and dealing with intimate and close relationships.

Thus, while these accounts of the 'stages of change' have made some interesting observations and began to explore the complexities of how people change their lives and how they overcome the obstacles that confront them, they appear in many respects to have serious limitations. They raise important, but largely unresolved, issues regarding the differences in the process of desistance in different groups and the impact of informal and formal interventions, as well as whether it is possible to develop a meaningful and consistent model of change. Most importantly, they do not present a coherent account of how people move from one stage to another, how and why they skip stages or engage in lapses and reversals. Although the stages or phases presented by authors such as Ebaugh and Mansson and Hedin are less rigid than those provided by Prochaska they remain 'ideal types' rather than a description of the process of change. Thus they are at best sensitising concepts, and should not be confused with the reality of the processes concerned.

Styles of change

Sanders (2007) takes a distinctly different approach to the process of exiting. Rather than present stages of change, she presents a typology of *styles* of change. She identifies four main styles that people might adopt (1) *reactionary*, which involves a reaction to a significant negative or positive experience, (2) *gradual planning*, in which change takes place over a period of time in response to a range of events and experiences, (3) *natural progression*, which may be the result of maturation or a strong desire for a different lifestyle, and what she calls (4) *the yo yo pattern*, which involves the frequent movement in and out of prostitution.

A similar approach has been presented by Cusick et al. (2011), who distinguish between *opportunistic* exiters, who are able to start and stop their involvement in prostitution in response to changing circumstances or specific events, and *gradual* exiters, who apparently reported accumulated changes over time or decided to leave prostitution as a result of maturity. The third group that they identified is *strategic* exiters. All of the members of the third group were involved in indoor prostitution and apparently were able to organise the conditions for exiting themselves.

These descriptions of styles of change, however, suffer from the same limitations as the stages of change models. First, the categories are not distinct, and in practice many women who are 'gradual planners' may leave suddenly because of a traumatic event or alternatively may engage in a series of lapses and reversals. These typologies may also refer to similar individuals at different stages of the process of change, rather than two different kinds of desisters. Second, and relatedly, because these categories are neither discrete nor consistent they have little or no value in terms of fashioning interventions and responses. Third, the theoretical base is weak, incorporating a peculiar mix of symbolic interactionism and control theory which aims to explore the structural constraints on exiting, while these approaches are best suited, as Sanders herself notes, to account for meanings, motivations and experiences.

Looking back: Moving forward

A central debate in the desistance literature relates to the need to overcome past experiences in order to move forward. That is, it is claimed by some scholars that in order to change their lives individuals need to 'knife off' what are seen as harmful experiences and undesirable companions. According to Sampson and Laub (2003), knifing off the past from the present is a central element in the desistance process. For Sampson and Laub, engagement with structural arrangements such as marriage, finding a job or going to prison provides an opportunity for individuals to develop new roles and identities. It is the engagement, they argue, with structurally induced 'turning points' that are seen to provide the basis for cutting adrift from the past and moving on.

In contrast, there is a significant body of work on prostitution that sees past experiences as playing an important role in relation to entry and involvement in prostitution as well as to exiting. A leading proponent of this thesis is Judith Herman, who in her classic text *Trauma and Recovery* (1992) claims that the effect of victimisation in early life leads to forms of insecurity, identity problems and the erosion of self-esteem. A consequence of these experiences, she argues, is repeat victimisation in adult life often accompanied by a sense of unpredictability and helplessness (Farley 2003). Consequently, she advocates the adoption of psychotherapeutic techniques to address the symptoms of trauma and to deal in some cases with post-traumatic stress disorder (PTSD).

Although this approach was very influential in the 1980s and 1990s, it has fallen out of favour in recent years (Swift 2005). While there is no doubt that a significant number of women involved in prostitution have suffered abuse and distress, it has been argued, particularly by some feminist critics, that Herman's psychotherapeutic approach reduces the social and political to the personal, and to the belief that all social and personal issues can most effectively be overcome through individual therapy (Kitzinger 1996). There is also a danger that the person concerned can become drawn into many years of therapy, which perpetuates rather than overcomes their dependencies.

In opposition to the approaches suggested by Sampson and Laub (2003) on one hand and Herman (1992) on the other, Maruna (2001) presents an alternative approach which argues that a person's past does not need to be a life sentence. Rather, he suggests that the aim is to develop 'redemption' rather than 'condemnation' scripts, which encourage people to make sense of their deviant lives and ultimately to develop a pro-social identity. Thus, rather than 'knifing

off' or dwelling on the past, the person is helped to construct a narrative in which even the most shameful past can be put to use to
provide a foundation for developing a more positive forward-looking
sense of self (Maruna et al. 2004). In doing so, the individual has to
explain to herself and significant others the personal change through
the reconstruction of her life history. Thus:

> Perhaps most importantly, ex-offenders need to have a believable
> story of why they are going straight to convince themselves that
> this is a real change. It is easy to say one is giving up drugs and
> crime. Yet, when setbacks occur – and ex-convicts are likely to face
> many such disappointments – wanting to desist is not enough.
> The individual needs a logical, believable and respectable story
> about who they are that makes it impossible to engage in criminal
> conduct without arousing guilt reactions and feelings of shame
> that are incompatible with the self-conception. The desisting per-
> son's self story, therefore, not only has to allow for desistance but
> also has to make desistance a logical necessity.
>
> (Maruna 2001: 86)

Rumgay (2004) has applied similar principles to the analysis of
desistance among women. She claims that successful desistance may
be rooted in a recognition of an opportunity to claim an alternative, desired and socially approved personal identity. Desisters, she
suggests, need to formulate credible 'scripts' which are linked to a
pro-social role. One of the difficulties of developing a pro-social role
is that many of the women in question may not have a detailed
familiarity with conventional scripts. Nevertheless, maintaining and
developing credible scripts is seen to be significant if the woman is
to avoid reverting to previous roles. This is why supporting relations,
both formal and informal, are important during the exiting process.
It also means that these pro-social scripts need to be worked on and
perfected, and this requires commitment and resilience on the part
of the woman.

Emotions and desistance

One of the important developments in the recent literature on
desistance has been an increasing focus on the emotional and

'existential' aspects of personal change. For many years it has been assumed that the application of certain forms of treatment would in themselves be sufficient. However, it has been realised that interventions only 'work' to the extent that they connect with the interests and capacities of the groups or individuals at whom they are directed (Pawson and Tilley 1997). In a similar vein, it is also suggested that the context in which interventions are mobilised can be critical to their effectiveness.

If we look, for example, at the range of interventions listed in Hester and Westmarland's (2004) survey of exiting programmes or Mayhew and Mossman's (2007) recommendations for 'good practice', we see that the main focus is on what might be identified as 'practical' or 'instrumental' forms of support. For the most part these involve a focus on drug treatment, housing provision, debt management and sexual health. Mayhew and Mossman (2007) add education, training and employment, and point out that developing trust and supporting relationships can be important.

Other studies of prostitution and desistance have given greater priority to the role of trust. Ward (2007), for example, in her evaluation of prostitution in Ipswich, argues that building up trust is critically important in helping women exit. Overcoming the mistrust that women involved in prostitution have, not only in relation to buyers and pimps but also to different agencies and organisations, is a necessary element of the exiting process. The re-establishment of trust is seen as a critical component to the re-engagement with family and friends as well as with the wider community. As Misztal puts it:

> Trust is a highly problematic but recurrent feature of social relationships.... For instance, it is seen as essential for stable relationships, vital for the maintenance of cooperation, fundamental for any exchange and necessary for even the most routine of everyday interactions. Without trust only very simple forms of human cooperation, which can be transacted on the spot, are possible.
>
> (Misztal 1996: 12)

Trust, it is suggested, is also essential for facilitating effective problem-solving, because it encourages the exchange of relevant information and determines whether individuals are willing to allow others to influence their decisions and actions. The person's emotional state is seen as important in determining whether more practical interventions, such as drug treatment and housing provision, are likely to be effective in relation to exiting. In general, desistance appears to be more likely when accompanied by a diminution in negative emotions and an augmentation of positive emotions (Farrall and Calverly 2006).

In a similar vein, considerable attention has been directed towards 'hope' in the desistance literature (Burnett and Maruna 2004; Farrall and Calverley 2005). Having hope suggests having a vision of an achievable alternative future. It signifies a positive intent to change. Thus it is becoming recognised that fostering hope and building up trust are necessary components of a successful exiting strategy, since these emotional developments are not only important in themselves but can play an important role in the effectiveness, or otherwise, of pragmatic interventions. There are other emotional issues such as guilt, shame and self-esteem, which all impact to some degree on the exiting process, but our understanding of how they work remains relatively underdeveloped.

It is also known that emotional development is linked to identity formation and that this in turn is sustained and conditioned by interpersonal interaction (Goffman 2009). A key component of the exiting process appears to be turning negative identities into positive identities. This can be achieved not only through individual motivation and the provision of different kinds of support but also through the mobilisation of 'identity politics', by which social movements can seek to alter the societal conceptions of stigmatised persons (LeBel 2009). Such a transformation was achieved in the 1990s in the UK when persons under 18 who were involved in prostitution were recategorised as 'victims' rather than offenders (Brown and Barratt 2002).

The important message from this growing interest in the role of emotional states is that rather than treating them as secondary or peripheral to the usual forms of 'practical' intervention, a greater emphasis on emotions and identity formation is likely not only to be a good in itself but also promises to make practical interventions more effective.

Conclusion

In this chapter we have critically reviewed some of the leading contributions to the literature on desistance and exiting. Although we have noted that there has been a growing interest in the exiting process, we have argued that some of the prominent approaches are deficient and in need of radical review. Therefore, it has been necessary to engage in something of a ground-clearing exercise which involves challenging some of the dominant conceptions and approaches.

In particular we have become sceptical of the various 'stages of change' models that have been presented, and suggest that they represent at best 'ideal types' of how individuals 'could' or 'should' go through the exiting process. We have also expressed some reservations about adopting a purely pragmatic approach, which maintains that the provision of drug or housing services, for example, will in itself be sufficient to facilitate exiting. Instead we have, in line with recent research on desistance, emphasised the importance of emotions and identity formation in the process.

In a similar vein we have questioned the notion that we need to develop a 'holistic' approach, which can provide a comprehensive response to the person's 'needs' linked to a multi-agency strategy. Again, this is something of an ideal type, which is some way from the lived reality of the women and agencies concerned. The identification of 'needs' is invariably selective and targeted while different agencies have their own priorities, diagnoses and strategies. It is also suggested, however, that any approach that aims to be 'holistic' will have to move beyond a 'deficit model' and consider the strengths, ambitions and capacities of the women involved, moving in the direction of what has been called The Good Lives Model. The implications of this ground-clearing exercise is that some of the familiar terrain now looks less solid, and that in investigating exiting from prostitution we are faced with the challenge of developing a modified view of the processes concerned.

2
Examining the Process of Change

Introduction

In this chapter we take up some of the themes and issues that have been raised on the literature on desistance and exiting and subject them to empirical examination. Based on a total sample of 114, which includes a smaller sample of 55 women who had exited at the time of interview, our aim is to shed some light on these contested issues. In doing so we focus first on the relation between structure and agency; second, the role of formal and informal supports; third, the relationship between past experiences and future developments; and lastly we examine the significance of lapses and reversals.

Structure and agency

One of the recurring issues that runs through the desistance literature is the relationship between structure and agency. Unfortunately, many of the attempts to explain either desistance or exiting tend either to gravitate towards a preoccupation with individual motivations on one hand or structures such as employment or marriage on the other. Although this debate remains unresolved, it is clearly the case that some consideration of both agency and structure is necessary – as well as the relevant mediations – if the issue of exiting is to be properly addressed and appropriate interventions developed.

There are questions about which comes first, agency or structure, and the relation between subjective and objective changes. Sampson and Laub (1993, 2003) have suggested that it is through a variety of 'turning points' such as marriage and employment that long-term behavioural change is produced, by allowing offenders to 'knife off' the past from the present and by providing new forms of social attachment and commitment. These 'turning points' are seen as 'triggers' which can change the direction of people's lives (Carlsson 2012; Laub and Sampson 2006).

The problem is, however, that these turning points are not randomly distributed and that different turning points may have a different impact depending on the motivation and predisposition of the people involved. Thus, there is no necessary relation, for example, between getting married and/or finding a job and desistance. Much depends on the nature of the marriage and the type of job. Moreover, these turning points do not just 'happen' but are usually actively sought by the person concerned (Giordano et al. 2002; Maruna 2001). However, as Archer (1995) has argued, structures do have a temporal autonomy and both pre-date and postdate the action sequences that reproduce them. Additionally, she argues in line with Sampson and Laub (1993) that structures have emergent and causal properties that are not reducible to the actions of individuals. Consequently, she maintains in contrast to Giddens' (1979) 'integrationalist approach' that it is possible to factually distinguish structure from agency because of the time element involved (Farrall and Bowling 1999).

The important point is that structures may or may not be turning points, although they may have causal effects, while turning points can be 'events' that are independent of structures. The implication is that not all those who engage in marriage or employment will leave prostitution but these forms of engagement will almost certainly influence their involvement in prostitution to some degree.

At the same time, certain subjective elements such as hope, shame, the level of remorse, the experience of stigma and the potential for developing alternative identities have all be found to affect desistance (LeBel et al. 2008). Giordano et al. (2002) have attempted to integrate these internal and external processes while identifying the gender differences associated with desistance. Adopting a symbolic interactionist perspective, Giordano and her colleagues aim to emphasise the creative aspects of change, while recognising the role of different turning points or what they call 'hooks for change' as catalysts for change. Although Giordano et al. (2002) suggest that the process of desistance is largely similar for both men and women, they do claim that the process of desistance is often quicker for women and that pregnancy and maturation can be effective 'hooks for change'.

In the course of our analysis we attempted to separate as far as possible the role and effects of the different processes involved. For this task we focused mainly on the 55 women who had exited at the time of the interview. In relation to 'structures', we found that eight women said that they left prostitution because they had begun a new steady relationship, four women cited becoming pregnant as a major reason for leaving prostitution, while three women left because they found alternative sources of income. In addition, three women in our sample decided to exit following their involvement with the criminal justice system.

Those women who left prostitution because they found a new partner tended to leave relatively quickly, since the women felt that having a relationship with a new partner was incompatible with their continuing involvement in prostitution. As one woman stated:

> I knew that he would be really hurt if he knew that I was doing that while I was with him. So it was a little bit hard to stop doing it because of the money, but the guilt I felt was bigger than anything else.

Becoming pregnant was identified as the 'turning point' for four women involved in the sample. One woman who was involved in escorting reported that although she had some reservations about her involvement in prostitution, referring to it as a 'degrading job', she decided to exit when she became pregnant.

> A lot of my friends stopped the industry... their whole mindsets changed completely, a bit like I am feeling now. Unlike those I didn't have a specific reason like falling in love but I found out I was twenty weeks (pregnant) and then I thought that things have got to change.

Three women in our sample left prostitution because they found alternative sources of income or employment. One woman was encouraged by her sister to move out of prostitution into drug dealing, which she was told was a more lucrative activity. She said:

> So I sort of told her what I was doing and she goes 'that's wrong'. She goes 'Let's get you out of that system and I'll get you a way to get proper cash'. And so I got into selling drugs. She got raided anyway, my sister did, and I took the blame and that because of her children.

Another woman, who had worked as an escort for nine years, set up a hair and beauty business. She had tried an office job that she disliked, and then decided to go on a course in order to be able to start her own business. She stated:

> Well I actually got a job just like a little office job really, but I didn't like it in there because I just didn't like the people there at all. So again it just reminded me of when I got into it (escorting) in the first place. So that's why I started my new company because I thought 'Well at least I have only got myself to answer to' you know. I just thought 'let's retrain and do something for me'. So that's why I've done my new business. I've actually created something that I really like.

The third woman found employment in a furniture shop. She had been involved in prostitution for 17 years and decided to leave after coming out of rehab. She found secure accommodation and a job with the help of her ex-partner. Significantly, all three women had taken some steps to exit prostitution before finding a job or alternative forms of income. In two cases they had already begun to reduce their involvement in prostitution or had taken steps to explore alternatives. Thus it was not the case that employment acted as a 'trigger' allowing them to exit, but rather that they sought alternative forms of income while they were already looking for a way out.

Three women exited after being involved in the criminal justice system. One left after receiving a prison sentence, the others left after receiving an Anti-Social Behaviour Order (ASBO). One woman had been involved in acquisitive crime, drug use and prostitution for a number of years and had been in prison a number of times, but decided to exit during her last prison sentence during which she accessed treatment for her drug addiction. She said:

> When I was in prison I thought, you know what, I am going to try this time because I need to do something. I can't go back out there to the life I have been living. I went into treatment luckily for me, it actually worked because it didn't work for everybody.

While for many women involved in prostitution criminal justice interventions tend to reinforce their marginalisation, and consequently their involvement in prostitution, in this case receiving effective drug treatment in prison helped her exit.

In a similar way, two women who received ASBOs managed to exit. At the time of receiving the ASBOs both women were extremely upset, since besides anything else it created difficulties accessing services in the areas in which they lived (Sagar 2007). By the time the ASBO expired they had both decided to exit. As one woman explained:

> 'Cos as you said, when I first got the ASBO I was just going to go back out there, nobody was going to stop me. But now I don't know if I am going to do that...I think it is 'cos I don't want to be out there any more. You know it is not a very nice thing to do.

It was not the deterrent effect of these forms of punishment that persuaded these women to exit prostitution but rather a forced change of lifestyle, and in one case gaining access to effective treatment. Gaining some personal and social space also seemed to be important in changing the direction of their lives. Apart from these structural shifts, some women identified other turning points that propelled them towards exiting. These included experiencing serious incidents of violence, maturation and an increasing inability to manage intimate sexual encounters.

Many women who were interviewed reported experiencing violent incidents, but in some cases these incidents were extreme and life-threatening. Eight women stated that it was directly as a result of experiencing an extreme form of violence that they decided to exit. One woman made her decision after being stabbed on the street. Another woman, who had been involved in street prostitution for four years, described the incident that persuaded her to leave prostitution:

> A kid pulled a knife, a big knife, to my throat and raped me...I think that's when I turned, when I wanted to stop and that's when I was really determined to get off.

This woman had made a previous attempt to engage in treatment for opiate dependency, but she felt that the support she received was inadequate. Although she had been thinking about exiting, it was not until she experienced this episode of sexual violence that she decided to 'get off', as she put it.

Another woman, who had been involved in street prostitution and had accessed support services on and off for a number of years, continued to be involved in street prostitution until she had an experience which motivated her to leave:

> This is what made me say that's it. A guy tried to strangle me and gave me a black eye. That's when I said 'That's it'. I haven't been out since.

Some women who experienced extreme forms of violence complained about what they saw as a lack of police protection:

> I got stabbed seven times and when I went to the police they didn't care. Basically, I'm a user and a whore and it was done by other users and whores. 'Get on with it and kill yourselves', that was the kind of attitude that I got from the police. That's what made me realise that you know what I'm better than this...I had to come out of this, I had to leave.

Women involved in prostitution, it became clear, tend to experience violence from a number of different sources – partners, pimps, punters as well as strangers and associates. Four out of five of the exited sample mentioned in their transcripts that they had experienced violence during their involvement in prostitution. Many of the women had experienced violence from more than one source, while for some the experience of violence was a regular feature of their lives. Thus from the sample of women who had exited, 23 had experienced physical violence from their partners, 11 from their pimps, 25 from buyers, and a further 34 from a family member, stranger or associate, while 22 of the women in the main sample also reported experiencing sexual violence from buyers. These figures suggest that the focus on violence solely from buyers is limited, and that if the issue of violence against women involved in prostitution is to be addressed then a much wider range of sources needs to be examined (Church et al. 2001; Kinnel 2006).

A recurrent theme in the interviews was an awareness of ageing, and a sense that involvement in prostitution over time had taken its toll on the women's health and worn them down both physically and emotionally. As one woman who was involved in street prostitution explained:

> I've made so many mistakes and the same mistakes over and over again that I'm just tired of it now, you know? I don't want to be making the same mistakes again. I don't want to be hating myself and feeling rubbish about myself any more. I'm sick of it. So, because I've been doing it for so many years now I'm ready for the change now.

Another woman who had also been involved in street prostitution stated that:

> It's just getting hard out there, you know what I mean? And I'm thirty-three now and I've got no qualifications. I've not done much with my life and I just want to do something different now.

A number of women said that they decided to exit prostitution when they realised that they could not manage the situation any longer; that buyers were beginning to repulse them and they could no longer sustain the motivation to sell their bodies for sex. Although in many of these cases the disillusionment or revulsion had probably been building up for some time, there appears to have been a moment or a particular experience that made the woman concerned decide to exit. One example is a woman who had been involved in indoor prostitution for many years who just walked out one day. She had no alternative form of income but decided that emotionally she could not do it any more. She said:

> I just couldn't bear to be touched. I just thought 'I can't carry on doing this no more. This is actually killing me this is. No amount of money is gonna make me feel all right after this day.' I didn't actually think I was exiting for good, because that's quite a scary process.

She added:

> I smelled of the guys and I smelled of the oil and I smelled of the talc.... I was like having panic attacks and crying and just in an absolute state. I felt I'd absorbed all the men's crap as well and I just felt disgusting and I was smoking absolutely loads of weed. I was paranoid and psychotic and in a really bad place, a really bad place.

After leaving she went on to have a breakdown and required medical intervention, but eventually managed to get in touch with a support service to help her work through all the issues that had been building up during her time in prostitution. These accounts draw attention to the emotional difficulties that many women involved in prostitution face, and the problems that they have managing the interpersonal and physical demands involved in providing commercialised sexual services.

Informal and formal support

One of the important mediations between structure and agency is the type and quality of support that women leaving prostitution were able to access. As noted above, many women have left street prostitution in Glasgow over the past 15 years with limited involvement with the formal support agencies (Matthews and Easton 2011), while in Ipswich the removal of street prostitution involved active engagement in the relevant agencies by the women concerned (Poland et al. 2008).

Hedin and Mansson (2003) have raised the related question of which persons or agencies positively influence the course of the 'breakaway' and what kinds of relationships and strategies are most important in helping women in prostitution construct a new life. They argue that reconstructing and strengthening family and social networks can be a determining factor in facilitating a person's ability to get out and stay out of prostitution. In some cases this involves re-establishing relations with estranged family members and in other cases finding new friendships or partners.

It may be a function of the fact that most of our sample of 55 women who had exited were accessed through various support agencies that only 11 women were identified as 'self-exiters'. Six women, however, said that their existing or new partner had been instrumental in helping them exit, while three said that their family was key to their ability to leave prostitution. For those who reported that it was the support that they received from formal agencies that was critical to them exiting prostitution, five claimed that it was drug treatment that played a major role in helping them exit, while seven identified housing as a key factor in the process. The remainder were unable to identify a primary factor, and said it was a combination of formal and informal support that had worked for them.

'Self-exiters' refers to those who said that they were able to exit either because they became increasingly disillusioned with selling sex or as a direct result of a frightening, traumatic or disturbing experience. The term 'self-exiter', however, requires some clarification. Although most of these women had some contact with formal support agencies, either these agencies did little to help them leave or alternatively, if they had been receiving help with drug treatment for example, they did not see this ongoing treatment as key to their decision to exit. Rather, they attributed their ability to exit to a high level of personal motivation, often coupled with some support from family and friends.

One woman who had been involved in prostitution since she was 18 decided to exit shortly after meeting a new partner. This new relationship exacerbated her growing revulsion towards buyers, while her involvement in prostitution created tensions between herself and her new partner. She explained:

> It's not like a single event. It's just a whole heap of things that have just made my mind up that I don't want to do it any more. Yeah, but it's just mainly I've got a boyfriend. It's killing me inside. I'm

getting sick of it, having to see these guys, do things that I don't want to do. And yeah, to sum it all up, basically when I'm doing this work I feel like I'm getting raped. Not because they are raping me. I'm giving them permission to do it. But every time they touch me, when they're inside of me, when they are doing things to me. It's getting to the point where I can't even stand my boyfriend touch me 'cos I'm associating it to work…I freeze up. I tense up when they touch me. I don't like it.

The self-exiting group tended to include women who had fewer personal and physical barriers to overcome and greater social capital. Some self-exiters claimed it was a particular incident that made them leave, although in some cases these incidents were the endpoint of a series of similar, although maybe less traumatic, experiences.

Those who identified formal modes of support as critical in their ability to exit were distinguished from the self-exiters by the fact that they identified receiving drug treatment, accessing stable housing and becoming debt-free with the help of specialist agencies as critical to their ability to exit. These women not only tended to engage in services in a more systematic and intensive way than those who relied on informal supports, but their engagement with the agencies and services was more likely to be linked to an attempt to overcome their perceived barriers to exiting.

One woman who had tried unsuccessfully to exit in the past explains how she eventually decided to do it for herself, and was able with some formal support to leave prostitution:

I just, I don't know what it was, something just changed in me and I wanted to reach out for better things and I tried many, many, many times over the years to do a program of methadone or I did codeines and I always failed because I was trying to do it for somebody else. But the minute I did it for myself, and the methadone, then I started to be on my way to recovery. And it's not been an easy journey. I have had slip-ups along the way but in general, if I even may say so myself, I've done extremely well.

Amongst the women in our sample, some 73 per cent of the women who had exited stated that they had accessed drug treatment services at some point, but there were remarkably few who felt that stabilising their drug use or stopping it altogether had been the primary reason for their exiting prostitution. Either coming off drugs or reducing their dependency on heroin or crack cocaine was seen by many as a necessary but not sufficient condition for exiting. A good number who received drug treatment continued their involvement in prostitution for some time, and it was the case for some that their drug use was more of a symptom of their involvement in prostitution than a cause. While it may not be the case that drug treatment is the main factor that allowed women to exit, it does appear that reducing drug dependency allowed some women to take greater control of their lives and make more considered decisions.

The possibility of these women moving from an initial interest and awareness of exiting to taking positive action is to some extent dependent on their having the opportunity to make contact with relevant agencies that provide appropriate support in relation to exiting:

> It's definitely about when you are ready but what's most important is having the option, I think, you know, as long as you're aware that you've got that option to get out of it then, you know, it makes it a whole lot easier.

Engaging with different support and treatment agencies can provide women who want to exit with an opportunity to develop a strategy to overcome the obstacles that confront them. One woman who had been involved in street prostitution was able, with support and guidance from a dedicated exiting service, to identify the obstacles that she faced and to realise that they were not insurmountable. She explained:

> I did really, really good. I spent a few hours essentially with [support worker] doing my exiting plan, which was fantastic, it really was. I've had to think 'Oh I need to do that' but then that would remind me of something else that I needed to do, that I wanted to do. And it just really helps to separate them all and put it into some structure. And they're all achievable as well, which helps.

Even if women are not able to exit after receiving formal support, whether it be in the form of drug treatment, housing provision or debt management, for example, it is the case that some women are able to reduce their involvement in prostitution and begin to address other issues. However, it was the case that such support was often instrumental and reactive, with few agencies that we encountered actively promoting exiting. Women reported that rather than dealing with women in a holistic, integrated and coordinated way, most agencies 'signposted' women to a range of agencies that dealt with specific issues rather than the whole person.

A significant number of women who had exited said that they had relied on a combination of formal and informal support. The formal support helped them overcome certain barriers, while family and peer support provided reassurance and the positive encouragement that they needed in order to exit. Thus it would seem appropriate that formal agencies should do more to link up and to foster available informal supports in order to widen and deepen the support base, particularly with significant others who are not associated with the sex trade.

Although we did not ask women how long it took them to exit from 'first doubts' to leaving prostitution, it is clear that many of the self-exiters left relatively quickly, while for those for whom exiting was an outcome of formal intervention it normally took longer. There were a few women in our sample who needed more intensive and longer-term support to exit, but it is remarkable how resilient and self-directed many of the women interviewed for this research were, given the difficulties they faced while they were involved in the sex trade.

What is clear from the review of these women who have exited is the central role that others play in instigating and sustaining change. As we have seen, significant others provide the impetus to shake off the heritage of the past and allow or encourage the women to commit to a future ideal. As Vaughan (2007) has argued, desistance is an intrinsically moral and cognitive process. For the person to exit they have to come to realise that being involved in prostitution is morally incompatible with whom they wish to be. This observation suggests that simply providing support services on their own is unlikely to be very effective in helping women exit, and that people need to undergo an 'internal narrative' of change that is supported and sustained by others if they are going to leave prostitution. Developing and implementing an approach that deals not only with the provision of the standard but necessary services such as drug treatment and housing but also includes more emotional, peer and community forms of support may well reduce the average period of time that it takes women to exit.

Forgetting the past and inventing the future

What is the relationship between the past and the future? Do people have to deal with and overcome past negative experiences in order to change their lives? These two questions are at the heart of the issue of desistance. For writers such as Herman (1992), engagement in prostitution is seen largely as a function of childhood abuse, neglect and associated traumas. Herman claims that many women involved in prostitution suffer from personality disorders and develop a stigmatised negative identity, which results in 'shame and mistrust', which in turn produces a pattern of 'intense, unstable and highly conflictual relationships' (Herman 2003: 6). This syndrome, Herman suggests, creates a framework in which women who are involved in prostitution come to believe that only a limited number of roles are possible – a perpetrator, an accomplice, a bystander and a victim, or perhaps a rescuer. Significantly, she sees excessive drug use not so much as the cause of prostitution, but rather as a coping mechanism to deal with the pressures and trauma. The implication is that dealing with drug use on its own is likely to have a limited effect.

A key component of the trauma model is dissociation. The impact of dissociation, it is claimed, both serves to propel women to prostitution but also permits psychological survival by providing an elaborate escape and avoidance strategy that involves a fragmentation of the self that is able to observe, experience and react to events. Paradoxically, the process of dissociation increases the risk of further victimisation, since the woman tends to dissociate in response to actual danger cues. Thus the psychological device of splitting the self into many parts, it is suggested, can involve forms of amnesia, depersonalisation and derealisation. Thus:

> A primary function of dissociation is to handle the overwhelming fear, pain and to deal with the encounter with systematized cruelty that is experienced during prostitution (and earlier abuse) by splitting that off from the rest of the self. Dissociation also reduces internal conflict and cognitive dissonance. The

dissociative solution to prostitution is an extreme version of the denial that occurs daily in all sectors of society: Bad things are ignored, or we pretend they will go away, or we will call them by another name.

(Ross et al. 2003: 206)

The treatment for dissociation and accompanying psychological and personal disorders is psychotherapy. This can only begin once the physical safety of the woman has been established, and it is suggested that both the client and therapist have to agree on the goal of ultimately leaving prostitution. The second goal of therapy is to establish a 'whole person perspective' rather than dealing with 'separate identities'. To do this requires addressing and overcoming past traumatic experiences, particularly childhood trauma. Not surprisingly, therefore, Herman (2003) suggests that the average period of therapy required to address these psychological and emotional problems is in the region of six years. However, as we suggested above, many women in a sample were able to exit prostitution relatively quickly, although it may have been the case that they still had some psychological and emotional issues to deal with.

In the course of the research we asked the women in the general sample about childhood sexual abuse and experiences of trauma and dissociation. One woman who had been sexually abused by her father's friend at the age of nine felt that her involvement in prostitution was inevitable:

You know it sounds like a cliché, but it was inevitable that I was going to go into the sex industry. I was taught that's what life is about. You know, sex for money.

Although this woman has a history of sexual abuse, her explanation of her involvement in prostitution was not so much as a result of trauma but a process of socialisation that equated sex with money. There were, a number of women who made reference to the process of disassociation. One typical response was from a woman involved in indoor prostitution:

I've got this ability to keep my head completely separated from my body. It's two different entities. Two different bodies and one does not interfere with the other. I do suspect that the way I was brought up, the childhood, would have facilitated that.

Another woman involved in escorting added:

> But I think genuinely switch off. I think that they call it dissociation, don't they? And they say that it's a bad thing, but then would it be a good thing if you didn't?

A number of women stated that they consciously adopted particular roles and were able to separate out their normal everyday selves from the self involved in prostitution. For some women this differentiation of the self was achieved through wearing particular clothes or using elaborate make-up.

> I think it's when I put my clothes and make-up on, I am [working name], when I take them off, I am [real name]. That's my work. When I get out, get my car, go to my house...I have a separate wardrobe in there for work and a separate wardrobe indoors...those two they cannot get mixed up.

Some women who had been sexually abused not surprisingly reported feelings of depression. For example, one woman stated that:

> I guess when I get a bit depressed sometimes, it magnifies that feeling of being damaged goods you know and that proves that, 'cos normal women without those issues don't go doing that to themselves, you know. But, other days when I don't feel down, I guess...I don't know it's just, something that I did. You know, part of the life...

Interestingly, this quotation presents an ambivalent, resigned and fairly philosophical response to years of sexual abuse, and although she sees herself as 'damaged goods' she was able to exit prostitution after receiving some counselling.

It is evident that some of the characteristics that Herman and others attribute to women's involvement in prostitution have empirical validity. Some 38 per cent of women in our sample had experienced sexual abuse as children, and some attributed their involvement in prostitution to these early childhood experiences. However, as has been suggested, child sexual and physical abuse is reportedly widespread in the population as a whole, and the vast majority of these individuals have not become involved in prostitution. This suggests that there are other important causal processes involved in the recruitment of women into prostitution (see Matthews 2008). Dissociation in various forms was also reported by a number of women as a coping mechanism, while drug taking also provided women with an effective way of managing this activity over time. Although there were some women who felt trapped by their past and could see no way forward, they were not the majority. What becomes evident when reading through the transcripts is that many women did not find it necessary to 'repair' the 'fragmented' essential self. Instead, they seemed capable of constructing a new sense of self and developing new roles and identities.

There were a considerable number of accounts in which women talked about blocking out the past either through the use of drugs and alcohol or some process of distancing and denial. One woman claimed she was able to block out her past experiences, and consequently was not deeply affected by her years of involvement in prostitution. She said she could not bring herself to prostitute unless she was under the influence of drugs, and could only do it in order to get money for more drugs. She considered herself fortunate to not be able to remember, and imagined that if she could then she would feel quite different. Reflecting on her experiences she said:

> I was just numb, as I say most of it I can't even remember which is probably a good thing, do you know I mean 'cos to have flashbacks and stuff like that would be it would be quite, you know, not very nice.

When asked if prostitution had any impact upon her, she replied:

> I don't really think it's had any to be honest with you. Not in my case, as I say, most of it I can't even remember, which for me is a good thing, I think because I didn't have any really bad experiences, and everything was just a quick at it, I don't think it really had.

Not experiencing memories or choosing not to have memories created a distance between her sense of self and her involvement in prostitution. Consequently she was able to exit relatively quickly and easily, once she had dealt with her addiction to crack cocaine.

While a number of women spoke about being able to distance themselves from the past and to exit without too much trouble, others seemed very capable of acknowledging their involvement in prostitution but instead of dwelling on the past were able to focus on the future. One woman who was involved in prostitution for one year as a teenager, in order to fund her drug dependency, said:

> I feel like, with the money and that, I feel like, I sort of put that out of my head. Really in one sense and that because I can't, no matter what happens, I can't go back and change it. I can only go forward and change myself. That's all I can do.

Other women shared this viewpoint, saying there was no point in dwelling on the past and that it was important to get on with life. As one woman said:

> You should really look towards the future and what can be done now, what can be done rather than what happened. I don't think there's a huge amount of point in going through everything that happened, I think it's very much sort of like getting a, a plan for life to change and thought of putting strategies, coping strategies in place.

Another woman, undertaking a 12-step programme, said:

> You know those things about myself that, my past is always been my issue and I'm at a point where I had accepted the past, and it's happened, you know. I know about it, but now it's dealing with it and I know that if I want to move forward I have to deal with it and all those issues that may arise when I'm at step four that may come to the fore.

She saw herself in the role of a wife and mother, and explained that it was because she wanted to get married that she had decided to exit prostitution once and for all. She was worried about what she was going to do for money but decided she would have to manage somehow, and built a new role for herself within the family as a wife and a mother. She had also been involved in charity work.

Another woman, who had exited from indoor prostitution due to exhaustion, claimed that she could not take it any more. After exiting she worked as a maid one day a week for a while. Despite her past experiences, she said she would not change her life as it had made her who she was:

> I just feel really happy now. I'm happy with my life. I feel really content. As I said I wouldn't change things 'cos I think it's made me the person who I am today and I think...It's made me more straight to the point now. It's made me kind of stand tall. It's taken me a while but I used to be quiet, not shy, but I used to feel the need to please everybody and I'm not that way any more.

Another version of the same response was provided by a woman who, although having serious misgivings about the period of time that she was involved in prostitution, feels that her experience has made her stronger:

> If there is a positive thing is that I've been there, I've been through it and I've come out the other end and I'm a stronger person than what I was then. I've got everything I've got now. So that's a positive thing, and I made a lot of new friends and people in society and, you know, as I'm going along with doing the training and learning all sorts of stuff so, that maybe I'd never have learnt.

We have presented a number of these accounts because they are at odds with the claims of some desistance theorists who maintain that if a person is to move forward they need to deal with a range of psychological problems before they can exit prostitution. Additionally, these accounts do not fit very well with the claims that people have to construct a coherent and plausible account of personal change that provides a sense of continuity from the old 'deviant' self to the new identity (Maruna 2001; Vaughan 2007). There was little evidence of such accounts amongst the women in our sample who had exited. Instead, they claimed in many cases that they were simply able to block off large parts of the past and to distance themselves from their involvement in prostitution. While it is the case that they might take a disapproving attitude to the past activity, none of the women interviewed reported constructing a personal narrative of change, but rather claimed to be able to effectively shut out a great deal of the past and embrace the future. It is almost as if the women described shedding a redundant 'skin' and replacing it either by reworking the original 'good' self or constructing a new identity.

A number of commentators have pointed out the way in which women involved in prostitution are able to separate a public from private self and to limit emotional involvement by placing limits on the encounter, such as using a condom, avoiding kissing and making certain acts or parts of the body inadmissible (Day 2007; Sanders 2005) In this way they aim to protect the essential self, 'the real me', from being invaded and destroyed (Hoigard and Finstad 1992). Thus many women involved in prostitution see their real or essential selves as being located away from their encounters with buyers (O'Neill 2001). Browne and Minichiello (1995) described 'self-programming', which involves 'switching off the true self and going into remote control mode or adopting a role'; while Castillo et al. (1999) stressed the ability of women involved in prostitution to look at the positive aspects of an experience that is otherwise unpleasant, which was common practice amongst all the women they interviewed in Tijuana, Mexico. Similarly Brewis and Linstead (2000) mention 'distancing strategies', which they claim enable the maintenance of self-identity beneath the public professional mask. This is achieved, they suggest, through the careful management of time and space, role playing and locating different kinds of sex in different geographical, bodily and symbolic contexts (Vanwesenbeeck 2001).

Cognitive psychologists have commented on the ability of people to block out past experiences of abuse, and refer to it as 'motivated forgetting' or 'misremembering'. This is not the same as forgetting but is an active ability to suppress disturbing experiences. It is noted that in a situation of isolation where the experience of abuse is not shared with others that individuals are more likely to be able to misremember such experiences. The ability to misremember has also been found to be linked to the process of dissociation, which in this context is seen as a positive coping mechanism rather than a form of pathology (DePrince et al. 2012; Epstein and Bottoms 2002).

How can we explain these experiences of exiting, which seem to be significantly different from those presented in the desistance literature? There seem to be three related explanations that might account for the particular modes of exiting reported by the women in our sample. First, quite a few of these accounts seem to suggest that engaging in prostitution was not really their decision but they were coerced, duped or pressured into the sex trade. This form of neutralisation allows the women to deny with some justification that entering prostitution was a matter of free choice. Some women claimed that they could have done something else if they had been given the chance. Second, most of the time they are engaged in an act, a performance, designed to manage difficult intimate encounters. This is not their real self but a facade or a character that is created in order to play out the scene. Third, and relatedly, the women have little or no emotional involvement in the act, except perhaps experiencing a degree of revulsion. Their involvement is largely pragmatic: it is not their needs and desires that are being catered for. This again is likely to allow them to block off to some extent the impact on their sense of self-identity. These processes of distancing and neutralisation are often played out against a background of violence, threats and abuse. In these situations many women are likely to consider exiting on a regular basis, which might explain why once women decide to leave they can in many cases do so relatively quickly – given the appropriate support.

Lapses and reversals

Moving out of prostitution is a tricky business. Whatever the incentives to leave, there are a number of factors that either make a permanent exit difficult or draw women back in once they have stopped. These pressures and constraints have been well documented. They include difficulties of changing lifestyle and giving up a network of acquaintances, the need for money and recurring forms of drug addiction, as well as other pressures.

A number of women in the main sample expressed considerable uncertainty and ambivalence when they had stopped for a while. One woman, for example, who had been involved in indoor prostitution, expressed anxieties about feelings of isolation. She said:

> I suppose I'm frightened. I can't really explain why, I just, I suppose I'm as frightened as I was when I first started it. I'm frightened to leave it, because it's become [sighs deeply] it is like a comfort zone. I doubt if that's because it is familiar or if because you are like a member of a little group once you are in it, because we all know like what each of us is going through without saying ... I'm frightened of losing that and not really belonging anywhere. Do you see what I mean? ... Like stopping the work but feeling I haven't really got anything in common with anybody else and then being stuck in no man's land.

Similar anxieties and ambivalence were expressed by another woman:

> What I'm saying is that I think I'm going to fail to achieve this self-sustain period because I end up getting dragged back into it ... It just seems too complicated to achieve. It doesn't seem possible ... Sometimes this is so familiar that it seems like the easiest option.

Making new friends and moving out of the liminal world of prostitution can be difficult. There is always the possibility of one's past coming up, and some women expressed anxieties about fitting into mainstream society. Even amongst those who had stopped for a time there were a number of pressures to re-engage in prostitution. Two of the main pressures appear to be boredom and the need for money. It is often claimed that selling sex is 'easy money', but many women come to realise that there are major personal and social costs involved. As one woman involved in indoor prostitution put it:

> You get so used to the money don't you. I mean you say it's easy money but it's not really 'cos I think mentally it does eat you away. You think it's easy when you're doing it but it's not really. It is always with you later. And I think it did mess up our relationship ... It seems like an easy option of making money but I don't,

looking back now I don't think it was. It catches up with you doesn't it.

For others the pull back into prostitution was the result of being recognised in the locality by ex-buyers. One woman who found a new partner and had a baby exited prostitution, but remained living in the same area for a time. She found that:

Because I have lived in the area where I did it, you know. I tried to go out you know, to do my thing to the day and I would still have people coming up to me for business and that, because that's what I was known as in that area. You know what I mean?

After having a son with her new partner she eventually moved out of the area in order to avoid unwanted attention. Similar difficulties were reported by women who had been housed in hostels that accommodated drug users and women still engaged in prostitution. In some cases these hostels served as magnets for drug dealers, pimps and buyers, and women reported that they were often exposed to a range of pressures to return to prostitution.

Many women reported lapses, and a number of those who had exited said that they had made more than one attempt to leave permanently. The level and consistency of support, both formal and informal, seemed to play an important part in this process. Thus there would seem to be an important role for support agencies in providing reassurance as well as helping women overcome the various barriers that confront them.

However, as Prochaska et al. (1992) have pointed out, when individuals relapse they rarely relapsed all the way back to where they began. Additionally their research found that despite the frequency of relapses, in a cohort of individuals the number of successes continues to increase over time. Unfortunately, relapses are seen as a sign of failure rather than the norm. The result is that service users can easily become demoralised. However as Hoigard and Finstad (1992) found in their study:

When people think of a 'relapse' (to drugs) or 'falling back' (to prostitution) they associate it with dramatic and fateful events; that at the first of relapse all hope is lost, all hope is already crushed and everything becomes as it was. This is a damaging notion. It can function as a self-fulfilling prophecy in which the woman and those around her expect that she is now irretrievably 'back in the life.' That's not how it is. The majority of women in our study who have turned away from their earlier lives have experienced relapses.

(Hoigard and Finstad 1992: 122)

Thus, rather than seeing relapses as a sign of failure and giving up on the women, more effort needs to be made to reduce the number, frequency and duration of relapses, and to work with the women to find ways of helping them get back on an exiting track.

Conclusion

It has become commonplace to claim that leaving prostitution is a process rather than an event. However, as we have seen in some of the above quotations, in some cases it may be the experience of a disturbing or particularly violent event that prompts the person to leave suddenly, even if they have experienced similar events in the past. However, the repeated emphasis on process tends to suggest that exiting is in most cases a long-drawn-out process. (see, for example, Hester and Westmarland 2004; McNaughton and Sanders 2007).

While lapses and reversals are not uncommon, the available evidence suggests that women can and do exit relatively quickly in a significant number of cases and that they do not need years of treatment or counselling to do so. One reason why it can take some time for some women to exit is because there are relatively limited support services that are geared up to facilitate exiting. In many cases the agencies that do offer support see their role as encouraging women to stay in prostitution rather than exit. However, the provision of more 'holistic' services that deal not only with the woman's perceived needs but also develop her strengths and capacities, coupled with an effective combination of formal and informal support orientated towards exiting, would almost certainly reduce the average amount of time that it takes women to leave prostitution once they have decided to get out.

The structures that appear to be most effective in relation to exiting are finding a new stable partner and becoming pregnant. These are, as they say, often 'game changers'. Involvement in the criminal justice system can also encourage women to exit, not so much because of the deterrent effect of punishment but more often because it gives women time to reflect on their lives and the opportunity to explore alternative lifestyles. Finding employment seemed to play a minimal role in persuading women to exit and rarely acted as a trigger. Instead, the few women in our sample who took up paid employment did so when they were some way along the exiting path. The limited significance of employment as a factor in exiting may be to some extent because of the lack of work experience, skills and qualifications of many of the women engaged in prostitution, but it also might be a consequence of a low priority given by agencies, even those providing dedicated exiting programmes.

The claims by Herman and others that many women involved in prostitution experience trauma and require years of counselling in order to exit seems only to apply to a limited number of women. Thus, while there are a number of women who are so emotionally, psychologically and physically damaged that they can see no way forward, they are the exception rather than the norm. Therefore, they should not be taken as the main point of reference when thinking about designing exiting strategies. On the other hand, the claims made by Maruna (2001) and Vaughan (2007), that in order to exit women need to be able to construct a coherent and plausible account of personal change that links the past to the present, do not fit very well with the accounts provided by the women in our sample who had exited at the time of the interview. In a significant number of accounts, women claimed that they could effectively block out the past and dissociate themselves from the self that was previously involved in prostitution and embrace the future. These findings suggests that the 'explanation' of exiting provided by these desistance theorists, like the stages of change models, may be more of an ideal type then a lived reality. Alternatively, they may be relevant to those men who are moving out of crime but do not apply in most cases to women involved in prostitution.

If our interpretation of these findings is correct, it suggests that the leading explanations of desistance that have been presented do not seem to apply to women exiting prostitution. It has been suggested that this is for three main reasons. First, people involved in crime, for example, are more likely to see this as an essential part of the 'self', while many women involved in prostitution become experts in constructing personae in order to manage buyers in the most effective way. In doing so, they have little emotional involvement, and consequently the essential self is bracketed off and can remain largely intact. Second, there is an element of neutralisation, inasmuch as the majority of women feel that they exercised little choice when they entered prostitution and that they were either pressured or led into prostitution by others. In addition, having to deal with people and do things that they find personally abhorrent, together with episodes of violence and abuse, provides a continual stimulus for women to regularly consider exiting.

3
Barriers and Opportunities

Introduction

The obstacles or barriers to exiting faced by women involved in prostitution are widely recognised. These typically involve drug dependency, homelessness, lack of skills training or low educational levels, together with poor employment histories. Other barriers frequently cited include financial issues and problems associated with physical and mental health. It is also widely reported that many women face a number of these barriers simultaneously, and having begun on an exiting pathway they often face a combination of obstacles. This is part of the reason why the route out of prostitution is rarely linear, since even when women have overcome one barrier they may be set back by others.

One study that focuses in particular on the relationship between exiting drug use is presented by Cusick and Hickman (2005). They claim that problematic drug use and prostitution – particularly street prostitution – tend to be mutually reinforcing. Although it is recognised that drug-dependent women involved in prostitution often have problems other than their drug use, the authors argue that for the women in their sample it is the pressure to earn money to maintain a drug habit that 'traps' these women in prostitution, and is therefore the main barrier to exiting. While there is no doubt that there are a number of links between drug use and prostitution that can be mutually reinforcing, the term 'trapped' in this context is disingenuous, since we know that the majority of even the most heavily addicted drug users will leave prostitution at some point in their lives, while some women who have overcome their drug dependency continue their involvement in prostitution The authors make no reference to the desires of respondents to leave prostitution, while the term 'trapped' as used in this presentation is itself something of a tautology, since if the women at the time of interview were identified as problematic drug users and were selling sex they were described as being 'trapped'.

Thus, in relation to exiting, this approach has little or no explanatory value. However, in the course of their article Cusick and Hickman (2005) raise a number of interesting questions about exiting. These include: (1) How central to the exiting process is drug addiction and drug treatment? (2) To what extent do background vulnerabilities affect the process of exiting? (3) Are there any particular combinations of factors that are particularly difficult to overcome? (4) Are there specific barriers which disproportionately affect the exiting process? and (5) Are there hidden or less visible barriers that have a significant impact on exiting?

In the course of this chapter these and related questions will be addressed in order to identify the different obstacles that women involved in prostitution routinely confront when they attempt to exit. Because many of the women face more than one barrier, and since they are often linked in practice, it is not always easy to identify the role of specific barriers. However, for analytic purposes we will endeavour to examine the role of different barriers as far as possible. Consideration will also be given in this chapter to the strengths and aspirations of the women interviewed, as well as the opportunities for change that they encountered.

Drug and alcohol use

The high prevalence of reported drug use in this and related studies makes this barrier appear an obvious starting point. Various studies have estimated that between 60 per cent to 95 per cent of women involved in on-street prostitution in the UK are considered to be problematic drug users (May and Hunter 2006; Ward 2007). In the course of the research, which sought to identify the relationship between drug use and involvement in prostitution, it soon became evident that drug use did not always precede entry into prostitution. For some women, drug use was a result of their involvement in prostitution and in some cases not the only or main cause of their continued involvement. Over a third (36 per cent) of the women said that they had become involved in prostitution before becoming heavily involved in drug or alcohol use.

However, just over half of the total sample of interviewees became involved in prostitution after becoming drug addicted, although some reported that the level of drug dependency significantly increased once they had become involved. Many women reported that drug use played an important role as a coping mechanism. Similar findings have been reported in other research (May and Hunter 2006; Surratt et al. 2004). In some cases it is not so much that the excessive use of drugs 'traps' women in prostitution, but rather the desire to give up drugs can be a basis for thinking about exiting prostitution.

Women involved in the study who were involved in prostitution at the time of interview were asked about their drug use, and their responses were coded into four categories – dependent, recreational or occasional, currently abstinent (previous usage) and non-drug user. Women who were involved in patterns of dependent drug use were those who reported daily use of drugs (commonly Class A drugs such as heroin and crack cocaine), women who were in drug treatment but continued to use Class A drugs, and people using non Class A drugs but in a habitual manner. Recreational or occasional drug users typically used powdered cocaine, cannabis and party drugs in a social setting but not on a regular basis. Among the women in the overall sample who were currently involved in prostitution, 67 per cent were involved in dependent or habitual patterns of drug use. Among women involved in on-street prostitution this figure rose to 90 per cent. Thirty-five per cent of those involved in off-street prostitution were identified as dependent and habitual drug users. Only 2 of the 48 women who answered this question who were involved in on-street prostitution identified themselves as occasional or recreation user, while 9 of the 20 women involved in off-street prostitution were involved in occasional or recreational drug use. A small number of women were identified as abstinent, and only three women involved in prostitution defined themselves as non-users: all three women were involved in off-street prostitution.

Seventy-three per cent of the women in our sample who had exited reported accessing some form of drug treatment while involved in prostitution. The type of support accessed included advice, group therapy, in-patient detoxification, residential rehabilitation and substitute prescribing. Although these different forms of drug treatment were widely seen as beneficial, reducing or stopping drug use did not necessarily provide an immediate solution for all the women concerned. Some women who were 'stabilised' on methadone, for example, continued to be involved in prostitution, while others required different forms of support and treatment in order to exit (Vanwesenbeeck 1994). Indeed, relatively few of the women who had exited reported that they had done so predominantly as a result of receiving drug treatment.

Indeed, our findings confirm the doubts expressed by some researchers about the significance of the role of drug treatment in relation to exiting (Melrose 2007). Although there is currently a large amount of funding and resources put into drug treatment services in the UK, the indications are that drug treatment alone is no panacea, and other forms of support or life-changing experiences are required for women to be able to exit prostitution. As one woman pointed out, the real benefit of reducing or stopping drug use was that it allowed her to think more clearly and improved her decision-making capacity. She said:

> You have to remove some of these chemicals from your body, so that you can think clearly. Otherwise you can't see no way out. While I was still in it and taking substances, there was no way for me personally.

This woman had been involved with support services for a number of years, but was eventually sufficiently motivated to exit following the murder of a close friend involved in prostitution. The fact that she was already receiving some treatment for her drug addiction to some extent provided a platform for her to make further change in order to exit prostitution.

Stakeholder interviews indicate that generic support services rarely identify as part of a routine enquiry whether the women accessing the service are involved in the sex industry. For those agencies that do not identify this client group, women in prostitution are unlikely to be asked if they would like support to exit. Indeed, it has been argued that drug treatment has been dominated by a narrow focus on individuals and their drug dependency and fails to address the social context and the underlying causes of problematic drug use (Buchanan 2004). By gaining a better understanding of the relationship between women's drug use and the involvement of prostitution, drug treatment services may be able to improve treatment outcomes. Assessments with women accessing drug treatment services should ideally find out whether women are involved in the sex industry, and if so what role drug use plays in relation to prostitution. Some consideration needs to be given to the consequences of removing this coping mechanism and whether there are other barriers to exiting which need to be addressed. By identifying women involved in prostitution, drug services are more likely to provide effective support, and are less likely to work on the assumption that drug treatment alone will be sufficient to enable women to exit. Decisions also need to be made about whether the provision of drug treatment is designed to help women cope more effectively with prostitution, or alternatively whether it is provided in order to help women exit.

In terms of the practicalities of accessing drug treatment, a study in Glasgow with women involved in street prostitution found that the women had a lack of trust in the support agencies, and that rather than dealing with the whole person drug agencies solely focused on addiction. It was also found that there was a lack of provision for opiate-addicted couples (Smith and Marshall 2007).

Housing

Access to safe and secure housing is well documented as being one of the most basic fundamental needs that women involved in prostitution experience. It is understandable that without an appropriate safe place to stay, to store possessions, have privacy or to make a home, there is little opportunity to lay foundations upon which to build a positive future. Much of the literature about routes into prostitution identifies the relationship between problematic housing and beginning to sell sex (Cusick et al. 2003). A lack of appropriate housing was also identified by some of the women involved in this study as a factor in their entry into prostitution, many of whom reported having had a history of unstable housing arrangements which had led them to sell sex to obtain shelter and to meet other basic needs (Sandwith 2011).

While housing and its relationship with entry into prostitution are a feature of the literature on prostitution, less attention has been given to how housing can act as a barrier to exiting. It is, however, becoming increasingly recognised that housing is a fundamental part of the exiting process. According to Mayhew and Mossman (2007), 'adequate provision of settled accommodation for sex workers is critical for finding routes out'. Farley and Barkan (1998) suggest that there is 'widespread evidence' that access to refuge and housing are key to the success of attempts to exit, perhaps as homelessness can interfere with the exiting process by undermining motivation, emotional well-being and self-esteem (Bindel 2006).

Stable housing allows women to feel safe and to begin to address other issues. It enables women to better engage and maintain contact with agencies and support services, offers respite or a resource for escaping violent partners and pimps, and provides a suitable home environment for women who want to maintain access to their children. Perhaps most importantly, good housing allows women to regulate access to their own space and to manage emotional and practical issues effectively. The type and location of accommodation and the support provided for women can also make a considerable difference to whether women will be able to successfully make this transition (Easton and Matthews 2012).

Owing to ongoing problems with housing, some women in our study stayed with buyers or pimps. This was normally for a very short period of time – perhaps one night or over a weekend. In other circumstances they stayed with buyers for a longer period of time, something that often involved more complex arrangements. In a number of cases women staying with sex purchasers or pimps were offered a place to stay over a longer period of time in exchange for sex and a simulated intimate relationship. One of the interviewees who was involved in street prostitution reported being evicted from her accommodation and moving in with a buyer. As she explained, he imposed certain conditions:

> At the end of the day he was a customer that I was living with and even though he wanted me to get clean and that was a condition that I was living there. Another condition was that I was having sex with him regularly. He was an old guy. I didn't particularly want to have sex with him.

In the interview, this woman described having resorted to this arrangement a number of times with different buyers, each time going back to the streets when it all became too much, until she eventually made a decision to enter residential rehabilitation.

Women also discussed their experiences in mixed hostel accommodation. Usually women resorted to this option when they had reached a crisis point or were picked up by outreach or enforcement teams. Mixed hostel accommodation proved for most to be a highly stressful environment, particularly as women involved in prostitution were frequently singled out and often experienced further exploitation or harm from other residents. Women rarely stay in this type of accommodation for long periods, often preferring to return to the street, or stay in crack houses, or enter into an arrangement with a buyer such as that outlined above. The desperation of this arrangement for women wanting to exit prostitution is illustrated in the following quote:

> I'm living in a hostel with all the working girls and junkies, and I hate it. Basically. But there's nothing I can do to change it, except wait to be offered a flat or commit suicide.

Research carried out in Glasgow indicated that the women's only hostels that cater for vulnerable women can have mixed benefits. For some women the hostel provided some respite from the immediate pressures that many women face on the street. However, some women living in the hostel experienced new vulnerabilities, and a number were drawn back into drug use and prostitution through associations developed while living in the hostel (Easton and Matthews 2012).

As opposed to the temporary accommodation options already discussed, some women were able to enter into more appropriate and more permanent temporary accommodation. This type of accommodation plays an important role for many women, allowing them to come off the streets or out of crack houses, but is often located in areas where prostitution occurs, making it difficult for women to separate themselves fully from the network of contacts which maintains their association with prostitution.

For this reason, locating women away from their areas of involvement in prostitution can help them exit, whether this involves sheltered accommodation, a hostel or some form of tenancy support (Ward 2007). As has been identified above, temporary accommodation for this group of women is often located in or close to areas of deprivation, often red light districts. Research by Dalla (2006) has pointed out the effects that living in areas notorious for drugs and on-street prostitution can have on women attempting to exit. In her study she found that those who had successfully exited had physically distanced themselves from other women involved in the local sex trade.

Women that we interviewed talked about feeling they would need to move areas completely in order to exit successfully. This acknowledges that the familiarity of surroundings, notoriety of an area for prostitution and the proximity of damaging peer groups can to a certain extent influence a woman's ability to make changes and attempt to exit (Dalla 2006). However, there are also risks associated with a complete break from familiar surroundings. This can lead to isolation if women are separated from their support networks and also from the comfort of the familiar situation, however damaging and negative it may have been. The analysis of women's experiences within this study suggests that breaking away in order to make changes needs to be balanced with having the ability to maintain positive relationships and support networks, in order to prevent women from becoming isolated or facing constant temptation to relapse (McNaughton and Sanders 2007).

Despite their high level of vulnerability, many women involved in prostitution will not fall within one of the priority categories for accommodation. Furthermore, admissions criteria, bed capacity and wait times can collude to deter women from accessing accommodation and prevent the take-up of this route to exiting (PAAFE 2005).

Serving a prison sentence or entering long-term residential rehabilitation may mean that women who have managed to establish some form of stable accommodation may risk losing it should they be sentenced to a period in prison of longer than 13 weeks. In addition to losing her accommodation, a woman also risks losing all of her belongings. On release such women are therefore vulnerable to homelessness, and may more easily fall back into prostitution as a means of survival. Furthermore, as one woman explains, the loss of personal belongings may have a significant emotional impact:

I've lost so much even the memories of my photographs, 'cos when I was evicted I wasn't around, I was incarcerated and the housing association took advantage and destroyed all my property, all my memories like my photographs and my certificates, all these … I had such a low point I couldn't even take the matter to court.

Providing suitable and stable accommodation for women engaged in prostitution has proved extremely difficult, particularly in a period of soaring rents and a general shortage of accommodation in many parts of the UK. One pioneering project, however, is the Chrysalis Project, which has been set up in Lambeth in South London. It has come up with an innovative approach to deal with some of the barriers women exiting street prostitution experience in relation to accommodation (Easton and Matthews 2012). The project is a joint enterprise between St Mungo's and Commonweal Housing, a housing-based action research charity.

Central to the provision at the Chrysalis Project is an approach that recognises the need to provide a variety of accommodation options that meet the differing needs of women at different stages of the exiting process. Women at the early stages of exiting are provided with hostel-style accommodation in a women's only hostel, allocated through the borough's centralised supported housing allocations team. Women at this stage are often extremely vulnerable and experience complicated mental and physical health issues, dependencies and other social challenges. This phase offers residential en-suite accommodation with shared catering and relaxing areas, and provides considerable support for women while also allowing increased levels of self-sufficiency. The project also provides emergency bed spaces (for up to 72 hours) for women who need immediate accommodation owing to their vulnerability or level of crisis. The second phase of the project provides post-treatment accommodation in one of three St Mungo's semi-independent housing projects in Lambeth. The post treatment accommodation provides en-suite studio flats for eight residents and a continuum of support around substance misuse, mental health and tenancy management.

Phase three provides women who have moved away from prostitution a tenancy in one of seven transitional move-on properties, with floating support from the same key worker. Women who move on to other accommodation are also provided with follow-up support. The accommodation consists of small, anonymous, one-bedroom flats in the borough. The project is unique in that the flats have been purchased and upgraded by a housing association and leased to Commonweal Housing. St Mungo's pays rent to Commonweal Housing, and any surplus rent is reinvested into the project for the ongoing provision of support.

This three-phase approach provides a number of benefits. It eases the bottleneck of waiting for local authority housing and it extends the support time frame available to women exiting, which allows them to further stabilise and establish more sustainable accommodation and employment options than they might otherwise be able to achieve. The three-phase model also provides women with greater opportunities for independence and supports them in maintaining their own tenancy and home, also giving them ongoing support for a short period after they leave the third phase and move on to full independence. An evaluation of the Chrysalis Project identified a range of positive outcomes for women who engaged with the project, particularly a sense of value and hope about their future and also a sense of privacy, independence and safety. In this way the Chrysalis Project provides a good model of how the provision of different types of accommodation at different stages of the exiting process can be critical in helping women move on and reorganise their lives (Easton and Matthews 2012).

Finding safety and having the opportunity to gradually make changes and take back control within a supportive environment are also seen as necessary components of Herman's (1992) recovery model. Others have indicated the need for women to learn the skills necessary to successfully maintain a tenancy (Matthews 2008). Thus providing suitable accommodation and the conditions for maintaining it can therefore be a key factor in helping women exit prostitution, and thereby helping them move on to a more independent existence.

Debt and financial issues

One of the recurring anomalies about prostitution is that most of the women claim that the main reason why they engage in the activity is to earn 'easy money', but most report significant levels of debt and financial problems. For those who are problematic drug users the money earned is mainly used to pay for drugs, and in some cases women support both themselves and their partners.

Debts include money owed to drug dealers, mortgage lenders, loan sharks, credit card and utility companies, as well as those run up by 'partners'. Debts were cited as one of the reasons why some women felt that they were not able to leave prostitution. Ironically, however, many considered that the fastest route to becoming debt free was to continue in prostitution. As one woman stated:

> I do see myself stopping very soon ... I would like to believe this time next year I'm sat here no more ... It's like my rent arrears will have been paid off by then won't they?

In this way many women appeared to be caught in a vicious circle of prostitution and debt. Although some women reported earning considerable sums of money, they also tended to 'earn it and burn it'. In some cases the money was used to pay for drugs, to pay off bills or was taken by pimps and partners, but in many cases women reported that the money just seemed to slip through their hands:

> I could take home two grand ... I slept with 29 men in one day. When you are working and earning lots of money you think that you need it, but because you are earning it in such a way you don't have respect for it, so you spend it silly anyway. I've always been crap with money .... You pay top whack for your drugs. You buy a lot more drugs than you need and you buy a lot of crap that you don't particularly need.

One interviewee who became involved in escorting in order to pay for her university course had intended to move on after a short time. However, she was sacked from her part-time job when it was discovered that she was an escort, and consequently she continued to work as an escort in order to pay her bills. She said:

> I couldn't give up escorting because I couldn't live on just the money that I had when I got sacked. I had to fund myself because my mortgage still needed to be paid, my bills and so I just decided

to keep with the escorting and at some point maybe I could try to do something else.

Although many of the women involved in off-street prostitution reported earning considerable amounts of money, much of it was spent on disposable goods, rent or mortgages, drink or drugs. In most cases they did not save or value money while involved in prostitution, and only registered the real value of money after exiting. However, both women involved on and off the street said that on one level the attraction of 'easy money' and the associated lifestyle provided a major barrier to exiting, while for some the lack of money after leaving prostitution provided an incentive to re-engage in prostitution, even if only temporarily.

One of the key services provided by support agencies is to put women in touch with debt helplines and agencies in order to negotiate the terms of repayment of loans. Some agencies provide managing money workshops in order to help women develop budgeting skills. These services, however, are limited, and it would seem that there is a need to develop a more manageable and comprehensive approach to debt management if we are to help more women overcome this particular barrier to exiting.

Criminalisation

The majority of women involved in prostitution live in a world of semi-illegality. Their immersion in this world has significant implications for their identity, vulnerability, social status, their opportunities to engage in legitimate employment and ultimately their ability to exit. In particular, their involvement in the grey economy places them in the middle of a deviant subculture that is likely to condition their involvement in crime.

Not surprisingly, many women in our sample had convictions for different types of offences, often acquired over many years. For the purpose of analysis, we separated these convictions into three types – those more or less directly associated with prostitution, those involving associated offences such as illicit drug use and possession, and thirdly what are often referred to as 'normal crimes', such as theft or offences against the person.

Nearly half of our entire sample (49 per cent) had a criminal record for prostitution-specific offences. The vast majority were, as might be expected, women involved in on-street prostitution. This is in part a function of the way in which prostitution is policed, with a greater emphasis on public order offences, having the consequence that women involved in off-street prostitution are less likely to come to the attention of the police (Matthews 2005).

Street prostitution in the UK is often identified as a nuisance and dealt with as such (Kantola and Squires 2004). In recent years there has been a concerted attempt by the authorities to 'cleanse the metropolis', in an attempt on one hand to appease local residents and on the other as part of a general programme of reconstructing inner cities (Hubbard 2004). During the twentieth century the aim of policing was to contain prostitution in certain 'red light' districts, but over the last decade or so the emphasis has moved from containment to dispersal (Beckett and Herbert 2008). The result has been both an intensification and diversification of policing strategies (ACPO 2011).

The major difficulty that the authorities have encountered is finding an appropriate sanction to deal with these public order offences. Imprisonment was removed as a direct sanction in England and Wales in the 1980s, and the fine has repeatedly been criticised since it is seen to put pressure on women to return to (street) prostitution in order to pay it off. Those unwilling or unable to pay off these fines are likely to receive a short prison sentence. As one interviewee reported:

> I've had fines – soliciting for the purpose of prostitution – and they wanna lock me up because I said I'm not paying no fucking fines to the government from my pussy money. Are you crazy? The government ain't gonna be my pimp.

More recently, women who have been repeatedly arrested for soliciting have been issued with Anti-Social Behaviour Orders (ASBOs), which place specific restrictions on the individual's behaviour and movement and if breached can lead to a prison sentence (Matthews et al. 2007; Sagar 2007). Issuing an ASBO to a woman involved in street prostitution can mean that she is unable to access support services. As one interviewee stated:

> I haven't been able to have any services – doctor or dentist. I can't even go to the hospital because I am ASBO'd from the hospitals. And it's not just one borough that I'm ASBO'd from. It's Camden, Islington and Westminster. You know what, Islington don't even

issue ASBOs. So how have I got an ASBO from Islington? And I've never been to Westminster.

ASBOs are due to be phased out and replaced by a new set of sanctions to deal with antisocial behaviour, including Criminal Behaviour Orders to be used to ban individuals from particular places or activities and civil Crime Prevention Injunctions designed to give agencies new powers to intervene in local communities. These measures, it would appear, are going to do little to address the problem of accessing support services, and look like little more than the repackaging of existing measures.

In recent years, however, women involved in street prostitution have come to be seen more as victims than offenders and more in need of support than punishment. Consequently, the number of women cautioned or convicted of soliciting and related offences has decreased considerably over the past decade from 2,111 in 2002 to 797 in 2011 (Home Office 2013). However, for those women who continue to be arrested and prosecuted for soliciting the impact can be considerable, both in terms of reinforcing their quasi-criminal status and by limiting their ability to find new forms of employment. It is for these reasons that some organisations are calling for the decriminalisation of soliciting for the purpose of prostitution in England and Wales.

The growing recognition that custodial sentences for women involved in prostitution can be counterproductive has led to the development of alternatives to custody, such as that introduced in the Policing and Crime Act (2009). The measures introduced were designed to break the 'revolving door' syndrome, whereby women experience numerous short-term prison sentences and re-engage in street prostitution on release. Under the new measures women apprehended for soliciting are given the option, following bail, of attending an initial assessment with a diversion scheme worker. Diversion schemes enable most women to be assessed and supported by specialist services offering help with practical issues, as well as exiting where appropriate (Rice 2010).

Although there has been a considerable focus on the policing of soliciting for the purpose of prostitution, we should not be led into believing that the removal of this offence will dispense with the issues of crime and social exclusion. Sixty-seven per cent of women in our overall sample had a criminal conviction for non-prostitution-related offences. Of these the majority were involved in on-street prostitution.

Thus, although the removal of the offence 'soliciting for the purposes of prostitution' would go some way to reducing the criminal status of a number of women involved in street prostitution, it is evident that a significant number of women involved in prostitution are also involved in other forms of offending. Due consideration needs to be given to the interrelated nature of these women's offending rather than treating it as a series of discrete acts. In this way, efforts need to be made to reduce the impact of criminalisation as a barrier to exiting.

Physical and mental health

There is extensive and detailed documentation regarding the sexual, emotional and psychological issues experienced by women involved in prostitution. Some of these problems are associated with intensive drug use, poor diets and lack of accommodation, while others stem more directly from their involvement in prostitution.

The emotional distress and destruction of normal relationships that women involved in prostitution repeatedly report suggest that the infliction of harm is a routine and fundamental part of the experience of engaging in commercialised sexual activity (Farley 2004; Hoigard and Finstad 1992). Women characteristically adopt various coping mechanisms for dealing with the pains and trauma of intimate sexual relations with strangers, including forms of disassociation alongside the regular use of drugs and alcohol to distance themselves from the effects of impersonal sexual encounters. Adopting these measures affects women's sense of self and identity.

An international study involving 700 women involved in prostitution in seven countries (Colombia, Mexico, South Africa, Thailand, Turkey, USA and Zambia) found chronic health problems, including tuberculosis, HIV, diabetes, cancer, menstrual problems, ovarian pain and hepatitis, as well as sexually transmitted diseases. In addition 17 per cent of these women reported mental health problems, such as depression, suicidal feelings, anxiety and extreme tension. Fifteen per cent reported gastrointestinal symptoms, such as ulcers, diarrhoea and colitis. The list of symptoms is extensive and reinforces the findings for other studies (Zimmerman et al. 2006).

These physical health issues were the result of a number of factors, including violence and assault by pimps, partners or punters, as well as poverty, which was associated with diseases such as tuberculosis. Physical health problems were also associated with intensive drug use, particularly amongst intravenous drug users. There are also physical and mental health problems that are more or less directly associated with involvement in prostitution, such as sexually transmitted diseases, hepatitis and gynaecological issues.

Women in our study presented a similar set of physical and psychological problems. Sixteen per cent of the women interviewed reported a physical health problem at the time of interview, while one in five women reported one or more mental health problem. The most common physical disabilities reported by the women were mobility issues. Twenty-four per cent of the sample currently classed their general health as 'poor' or 'very poor'. While over 90 per cent were registered with a GP, just over 60 per cent were registered with a dentist and a similar percentage reported that they had regular health checks.

In relation to their mental health, the women in our sample frequently reported depression and anxiety and other psychological problems. One woman, for example, discussed during the course of the interview how her ongoing involvement in prostitution was having an effect on her psychological well-being. She said:

> It's very damaging to myself... I don't like the fact that I'm standing on the streets. It's just not something that I want to do and I just can't take it any more. I really can't. I just don't want to do it any more... I freeze up. I tense up when they touch me. I don't like it. I just can't bear it any more. Then I always go back to it 'cos I need the money.

Some women felt that these problems were rooted in childhood experiences. Women, when interviewed, spoke at length about the range of abuse that they had experienced as children, and many felt that there was a biographical connection between this abuse and their subsequent involvement in prostitution. The literature on prostitution has drawn attention to the process of sexual revictimisation and the ways in which forms of victimisation experienced early in life tend to be played out in later life (Classen et al. 2005; Cutajar et al. 2011).

Those women who could not manage some form of dissociation found it difficult on one hand to manage purchasers and on the other to maintain normal sexual relationships. Women talked about their aversion to engaging in sexual relationships outside prostitution. They spoke about the general difficulties in managing intimacy, and some felt that they could not manage prostitution and a normal non-commercial sexual relationship simultaneously.

Our study both confirms and extends the findings of other studies that have looked at the problems of physical and mental health associated with involvement in prostitution. Many of the women in our sample said that they experienced these problems in different ways as both a barrier to exiting and a reason for exiting. The realisation in some cases of the physical and psychological effects associated with involvement in prostitution prompted them to take action and to limit or stop their involvement in commercialised sexual activity. On the other hand, some women felt that they were so 'damaged' that they found it difficult to see themselves forming new relationships and taking on different roles. Most women, however, had regular access to health services, and nearly all the specialist support agencies provided sexual health services or were able to refer women to such services. Thus for many women sexual health issues were seen as more of an inconvenience than an obstacle to exiting.

Education, training and employment

Two-fifths of the women in the total sample interviewed (39 per cent) had no training or formal qualifications when they were involved in prostitution. Women involved in on-street prostitution and trafficked women were found to be more likely to have no training or qualifications (49 per cent and 57 per cent, respectively) compared with 13 per cent of women involved in off-street prostitution. However, a significant proportion of the women interviewed felt that access to training and education were critical factors in relation to exiting prostitution. Among the women in our sample who had exited at the time of the interview, it was found that 22 had no formal qualifications, 11 had some vocational training, 7 had engaged in further education, 8 had experienced both further education and vocational training and 5 had secondary education.

Given that the vast majority of women involved in prostitution will move on at some point in their lives and take up a different occupation or activity, it is strange that in the extensive literature on prostitution there is virtually no reference to or discussion about what women do after leaving. In order to address this question and find out more about 'routes out', we asked the women who had exited at the time of interview about their experiences and activities since exiting. Amongst the sample of 55 women we found a mixture of roles, activities and occupations that they had taken up. These included becoming a mother, volunteering, caring roles, education and training as well as paid employment. A significant feature of the desisting participants in this study was that they expressed a strong interest in engaging in socially useful work with a strong 'moral' purpose, such as social work, working with children and various helping or supportive roles. As Maruna (2001) and others have noted, many of those leaving deviant careers become not merely moral but hyper-moral, and in some cases seek work and activities that have a purpose.

> I wanted to do something instead of just about me, and I think sometimes if you do something for others, even if things aren't good for you, it actually takes your mind off you as well and you know, you also see in the shop we had a lot of people with mental health problems coming in and a lot of people who were very lonely, a lot of little old ladies, people who were very vulnerable and I realised how quite lucky I was and I really enjoyed the work and I met loads of great people, loads, and I met lots of friends and that was good.

Of the 55 women asked about their roles after leaving prostitution only 48 gave a response. In some cases they adopted a combination of roles after leaving prostitution. For example, some women reported taking up a number of different roles simultaneously, such as looking after a new baby, moving in with a new partner and becoming involved in some form of paid employment. Thus for the most part we have tried to indicate the primary role, but the total number of roles reported is greater than the number of respondents because some adopted multiple roles after exiting.

The most common role adopted by the women who had exited was that of mother, with 18 women reporting that this was their main role after leaving prostitution. Eleven women either re-engaged with their children after leaving prostitution, while four left because they became pregnant and decided to look after their children full time. In two of these cases the fathers of the newborn babies were male buyers. One woman became full-time carer for her grandchildren. As Rumgay (2004) has pointed out, for an opportunity to desist to be seized it helps if it involves adopting a script which is both recognised and valued. She identifies becoming a mother as an example of claiming an alternative, desirable and socially approved identity.

Engaging in some form of education or training after exiting was the choice of 12 women. The most popular courses were IT and various vocational courses, including courses on beauty and fashion, with one woman planning to enrol in an undergraduate degree in social science.

In some cases the exiting process involved a combination of changing roles and activities. For example, in one case a woman's exit was prompted by her becoming pregnant, and this was followed by a desire to engage in training with a view to future employment:

> One day I just went to sleep and I woke up and thought about hair extensions 'cos I'd been wearing them for ten years. 'Why on earth aren't I doing this?' And so I went on a course and just trained in it and, you know, I'm back to another course next week. And it's just opened my eyes to like the normal life again, you know, it's just been a breath, it's just been a dream come true.

Six women said that they became involved in full-time employment soon after exiting. This employment involved jobs in retail, sales and office work. Two women became self-employed – one starting a new business and the other returning to a previous form of self-employment. Significantly, however, none of these women said that it was the offer or even the prospect of engaging in paid employment that was the trigger to exiting. Indeed, all the women looked for or round paid employment during the process of exiting or after leaving prostitution (Giordano et al. 2002).

These responses give an indication of the types of roles and activities in which women who exit prostitution engage. There has, however, been a lack of focus on what we might call 'through-care' in exiting programmes. Given the lack of education and work experience of many women involved in prostitution, greater emphasis needs to be placed on forming links to education, training and employment while women are in the process of exiting, rather than waiting until they have left prostitution.

Age of entry and exiting

The question has been raised in the general literature on desistance whether the age of entry into a particular activity affects the mode of exiting. Relatedly, the question has also been raised of whether the number of barriers that people have overcome affects their pathways of change (Cusick et al. 2003; Sampson and Laub 2003).

For our purposes we compared the routes out of prostitution with those who entered prostitution as children (under 18) with those who entered as adults. Clearly many of those who had become involved in prostitution as children experienced a different mode of entry and different decision-making processes in general than those who had originally become involved in prostitution as adults.

In our entire sample 35 women (32 per cent) first became involved in prostitution under the age of 18, with a slightly higher percentage of these involved in on-street compared to those involved in off-street prostitution becoming involved as children (33 per cent and 24 per cent, respectively). A comparison between the number of barriers faced by those who entered prostitution as children and those who entered as adults was revealing. It was clearly evident that there was a correlation between age of entry and the number of barriers experienced, with those who entered as children experiencing a significantly greater number of barriers than those who entered prostitution as adults.

Women facing multiple barriers felt that certain agencies do not understand how these barriers connect with and reinforce one another. What was significant about the process of exiting was that both those who began in prostitution under 18 and those who became involved after 18 were able to exit with relatively little support. In fact, more of the self-exiters were those who had become involved in prostitution under the age of 18, while the length of involvement in prostitution seemed to make little difference in itself to the exiting process. What appeared to be more critical was the level and quality of support, the degree of motivation and the impact of different turning points, as well as the effects of situational and structural constraints.

Thus, in line with Sampson and Laub's (1993) account of the relation between age of entry and the process of desistance, our findings indicate that many women who enter prostitution as children are still able to exit effectively. That is, 'routes out' are not determined by 'routes in', and there is a considerable degree of personal, social and structural variability in the exiting process.

It should be remembered, however, that just because women cease to engage in prostitution, they do not stop having health, psychological or other personal and emotional problems to deal with. Some of those who had a history of child abuse, exploitation or repeated victimisation may take many years to deal with these issues.

Coercion

One of the less frequently cited barriers in the literature on exiting is coercion, although the role of coercion within prostitution is becoming more widely recognised and definitions of coercive conduct are expanding. Women involved in the research reported coercion in a number of different forms. Most prominent was physical coercion from partners or pimps, and in some cases relatives. However, more subtle emotional pressure was also reported, and some women who found themselves continuing to be involved in prostitution out of duty, loyalty, fear or guilt, although they wanted to exit. The classic scenario was women who were pressured or threatened by their drug-addicted partners to keep selling sex in order to support their habit. Fifty-four women in our overall sample said that they had experienced some form of coercion while involved in prostitution, and that this had made it very difficult for them to exit. Significantly, 29 women reported being forced into prostitution by a coercive partner.

The issue of coercion was found to be a significant barrier in Ipswich. Although the various agencies were very effective in reducing the level of street prostitution relatively quickly and helping most of the women leave prostitution, it was found that:

> There have been reports of intimidation of women as they remain in the project by male partners or associates linked to drug use and the general risk to these women of physical, sexual and domestic violence appears high.
>
> (Poland et al. 2008: 79)

Finding ways of working with these men proved difficult, and suggested an overlap between prostitution and domestic violence.

Needless to say, all of the trafficked women interviewed had experienced coercion, ranging from the most brutal forms of violence to threats to endanger their families or more subtly to control them through deception and witchcraft. In an attempt to limit the 'demand' in relation to women who had been trafficked, Section 14 of the Policing and Crime Act (2009) inserted article 53A into the Sexual Offences Act (2003) and made it an offence to pay for the sexual services of a prostitute who is, or has been, subject to exploitative conduct by a third person. Exploitative conduct includes force, threats (violent and non violent), any form of coercion and deception. Significantly, the notion of 'coercion' has been redefined and expanded in recent years. For example, in the case of R v Massey (2007) at the Court of Appeal the judge stated that:

> There may be a variety of reasons why the other person does as instructed. It may be because of physical violence or threats of violence. It may be because of emotional blackmail, for example, being told that 'if you really loved me, you would do this for me'. It may be because the defendant has a dominating personality and the woman who acts under his direction is psychologically damaged and fragile. It may be because the defendant is an older person and the other person is emotionally immature. It may be because the defendant holds out the lure of gain, or the hope of a better life. Or there may be other reasons.

This pronouncement raises important issues about what qualifies as 'coercion' and indicates that many women involved in prostitution, apart from those who have been trafficked, are subject to different forms of coercion.

Strengths and opportunities

It is important when considering exiting that we do not dwell exclusively on the problems and obstacles that women wanting to leave prostitution often have to face. Many of these women, as we have seen, are forward looking, and those with a more positive outlook are more likely to exit in a reasonable period of time. This is why notions of trust and hope are frequently cited in the desistance literature (Burnett and Maruna 2004; Farrall and Calverly 2006; Ward 2007).

Some of the projects that have been established to provide support for women involved in prostitution have also come to realise the value of building up trust. An evaluation of the POW Project, for example, has emphasised the importance of trust, not just in their service provision but also as part of a wider social agenda:

> POW has previously documented the importance it places on developing networks, supporting [sex] workers, their friends, families and neighbourhoods in which they live. It has proven extraordinarily successful in fostering trusting, supportive relationships among its clients and those important to them. Network building and trust are key aspects of social capital, which has been linked to health and social cohesion. In the study reported here, workers who used POW were not only satisfied with the services provided but highlighted how much they trusted the organisation and how important this was in helping them make necessary changes in their lives.
>
> (Gillies et al. 2004)

In conjunction with considerations of hope and trust, the research also sought to identify the strengths, opportunities and aspirations among women considering exiting prostitution. For this purpose women in the sample were asked to complete a future mapping exercise, which formed the last part of the interview. The interviews with women in our sample incorporated questions that were designed to gather information about the women's future plans, hopes and aspirations and adopted a creative free-mapping approach similar to that developed by the National Treatment Agency as part of the International Treatment Effectiveness Project. The concept was explained to each participant and they were all then asked to create maps of their own. Many women found this a challenging experience, particularly those who were in more difficult circumstances or heavily entrenched in a lifestyle they were not happy with. Some women felt that the prospect of leaving prostitution would be too difficult, and they were not able or ready to envisage or imagine a different future.

The women approached the mapping exercise in a number of ways. Of those who drew a diagram, almost half placed themselves at the centre with their goals for the future around the outsides of the central section. One woman drew a diagram in the style of a timeline with her at the beginning, illustrating a progression through goals and decisions. Some women preferred to write down their goals for the future rather than draw a diagram or map. The women's drawings commonly contained the woman herself on the page with her family, partner or children, a house and the sun. The maps varied in the amount of detail offered, with some depicting more specific goals and areas that they wanted to focus on in the future, while a few women simply wrote personal messages, such as 'be happy' or 'live each day to the max'.

Although the maps varied quite widely in style, structure and content, there were some identifiable themes among them. The most frequently occurring theme was reference to family and friends. This normally involved having more contact or improving relationships with family members, friends or partners. Children in particular featured in future mapping. References tended to focus on strengthening relationships with children, being able to provide for them or gaining access to children who had been taken into care. For example, one woman who had been involved in the sex industry for 14 years described that she wanted to focus on her daughter who was approaching her teenage years, with one of her goals to guide her daughter through her teenage years and try to prevent her from 'making the same mistakes I did'.

References to housing were also a major theme. For example, one woman who had been involved in prostitution for over ten years drew a house and a pram, and presented herself as a housewife with a husband who was helping her to reduce her drug use. Dealing with drug addiction was another common theme. In the majority of cases the main objective was to be free from drugs, or at least to reduce their usage. An example was a woman who was still involved in prostitution, and had been so for over 20 years at the time of first interview. She had been in a children's home and was pimped into prostitution at the age of 16 by an older man, who also introduced her to drugs. Her goals were: 'to stop taking drugs and stop selling her body for sex, to sort her life out, find somewhere to live and go to college'.

A significant number of women wanted to start some form of training or go to college. Others expressed a desire to find employment, particularly involving a caring role. The types of employment that were mentioned included working with other women involved in prostitution, acting as a drugs counsellor and working with young people.

There were also women who specifically referred to their desire to exit. Two of the women outlined the different paths they could take. One woman who was predominantly involved in off-street prostitution discussed how she had reduced her involvement by not prostituting at weekends or during evenings, with a view to eventually exiting. She used her free map to draw out three possible choices and routes that she could take: to remain as an escort and then 'retire', exit prostitution and gain more qualifications in order to go into journalism, advertising or writing, or work in social services and then follow a more family orientated pathway, getting married and having children.

One woman who was involved in on-street prostitution used the map to encapsulate a number of goals with approximate time frames attached. For example, she wanted to leave prostitution in the next six months. In six to eight months she wanted to stop taking drugs. Within a year she wanted to go to college and do a course to enable her to retrain as a beauty therapist. Within two years she wanted to be reunited with her daughter. In four years she wanted to be out of London and working, and within six to eight years she wanted to be married and have another baby. Two women made references to support services in their free maps; they were both involved in on-street prostitution. Both of them wrote about their desire to continue attending meetings and accessing support.

A number of women mentioned 'happiness' as a goal. Five women referred to improving their emotional well-being, either in terms of increasing their confidence, how they felt about themselves or wanting to feel more positive. One typical response summarises the types of goals and objectives that many women sought while in the process of exiting:

> But now I feel that I'm moving on. The programme, relationships, volunteering, family, staying clean, and staying focused.

These findings are similar to the responses that Hoigard and Finstad (1992) reported in their study of prostitution in Norway. In response to a question about how they wanted to be living in five years, the women in their sample typically referred to engaging in education and working in professions concerned with people. Other forms of employment that were mentioned involved the development of skills that they had already picked up, such as hairdressing, being a beautician or working in retail. Other objectives involved establishing a secure relationship, having children or reconnecting with their family and kids. Thus, it would seem, the goals and aspirations of many of the women involved in prostitution are reasonably modest and achievable. Women do not talk about aspiring to great riches or a celebrity lifestyle. They appear to want a 'normal' life with a family and a stable partner, secure accommodation and a form of employment that matches their skills and interests.

Conclusion

The array of barriers to exiting faced by many women involved in prostitution can be considerable. What is remarkable about this situation is how women – even those with a history of abuse and victimisation – are able to effectively overcome these barriers. This is testimony to their resilience and perseverance: having made the decision to leave prostitution, they are in most cases able to exit in a reasonable period of time. Significantly, there is little difference between the mode of exiting between those who entered prostitution as children and those who entered after the age of eighteen.

Many of the women that were interviewed had experienced one or more 'instrumental' interventions, including drug treatment, housing provision, debt management and health care. In some cases these services were sufficient to allow women to cease their involvement in prostitution, but the evidence suggests that when these interventions were on one hand combined with informal supports and on the other the adoption of more positive, pro-social roles, interventions were more effective.

It should be noted that in some cases certain 'barriers' can also act as a stimulus to change. As we have seen, some women at a certain point come to realise that their drug dependency is damaging their lives and prospects, and as a result they decide to give up or reduce their consumption of illicit drugs. In some cases the relationship between drug addiction and continuing in prostitution becomes clear and they decide to try to exit. Debt and financial problems are similar: it becomes apparent at a certain point that staying in prostitution is only likely to increase rather than decrease their financial problems, and consequently they decide to cut their losses and try to leave. In this way the distinction between 'barriers' and 'opportunities' can become blurred, particularly when women come to realise that continuing in prostitution is likely to exacerbate rather than resolve their problems. Thus drug use and other 'barriers' are not always 'traps', but may provide a stimulus to change.

4

Exiting Among Women Involved in On-Street and Off-Street Prostitution

Introduction

This chapter concentrates more specifically on the different experiences of exiting reported by women involved in on-street and off-street prostitution. Previous research has identified some significant differences in the routes out for different groups of women, and has examined this in the context of differences in agency and structure (Giordano et al. 2002; Mansson and Hedin 1999; Sanders 2007). In the last chapter we examined the various barriers faced by women involved in prostitution as a whole. In this chapter the aim is to compare and contrast the different routes out of prostitution faced by different groups of women, and the different kinds of obstacles and opportunities that they encounter.

Barriers and strengths

In relation to the various barriers that were outlined in the previous chapter, there are some significant differences between the two groups that took part in our study, with a greater proportion of those women involved in on-street prostitution experiencing more obstacles to exiting in general than those working off-street. The type of prostitution that women are involved in will condition the types of exiting support and interventions needed. Immediate support priorities for on-street women identified by stakeholders tended to be centred on drug treatment and housing provision on one hand, coupled with building up supporting and trusting relations on the other.

Often women involved in on-street prostitution have personal and occupational histories that have caused them to lose trust in people and institutions. Rebuilding trust where there is no history of trusting relationships presents a major challenge. As one woman explained:

> You lose trust with people. I say I'm a people person but when you've been abused since you're a small child and been exploited you do become weary and it takes you a lot to trust somebody, but once you start to trust everything opens up more. I can't explain, it but it opens more doors.

The loss of trust can also be increased by a series of negative experiences that women frequently encounter while involved in prostitution:

> I used to be really trustworthy with anyone, but now I'm like: 'Hang on, let me think again,' ... meeting new people, I'm wondering if they're going to thieve off me, stab me in the back because it's what other users and whatnot have done.

For off-street women, exiting tends to be more focused on emotional shifts and changing feelings about their involvement in prostitution. While this group also requires practical support, the most prominent aspect of exiting tends to be centred on their self-motivation, particularly when faced by a peer group which for various reasons is generally unsympathetic. One woman involved in escorting spoke about this emotional shift and the difficulties it presented when she was exiting:

> It was quite difficult 'cos a lot of the girls around me were still kind of the happy hooker brigade ... So I was just like 'Oh I really want to stop doing this job, it's so horrible ...' It was difficult because of other people's reactions trying to keep you in, because obviously they are quite unhappy, they don't want you to be happy in a way, do they? It's like peer pressure.

Adopting a persona or different identity in order to engage in prostitution was particularly prominent amongst the off-street sample. In contrast for women involved in on-street prostitution, discourses around exiting tended to centre on 'moving on' and making alternative personal and social arrangements.

One of the few studies that has provided a comparison between the characteristics of on-street and off-street women involved in prostitution is that by Jeal and Salisbury (2007), which involved 142 women equally divided between those working on-street and off-street. Although they were mainly concerned with the health needs of the women they interviewed, their research also contained information on the backgrounds of their respondents, their mode of entry into prostitution and their different working practices.

The main differences that they found were that those working off-street were less likely to report chronic illnesses and were less likely to use heroin or crack cocaine. They also reported more stable childhoods, a lower level of child abuse, lower rates of homelessness, and claimed that they were less likely to be drug addicted or experience serious health problems. Overall, the picture that Jeal and Salisbury (2007) paint is that the women involved in street prostitution are more at risk, more unstable and generally more problematic than those working indoors. However, our research indicated that these differences were not as great as Jeal and Salisbury suggest, and that off-street prostitution is in some respects just as problematic as street prostitution. If we look, for example, at the issue of drug use, we can see that while women working on street were more likely to be using heroin and crack cocaine, women working indoors also engaged in a significant level of 'problematic' drug use.

Drug and alcohol use

Jeal and Salisbury (2007) reported that only 6 per cent of women working off-street used heroin compared to 85 per cent of those involved in on-street prostitution, and that only 7 per cent of those working indoors compared with 87 per cent of women engaged in street prostitution used crack cocaine. None of the women working off-street were reported to have used benzodiazepines, but one in four said that they used cannabis. Thus, Jeal and Salisbury (2007) suggest that drug use is much more prevalent amongst women involved in street prostitution, and they add that this group is much more likely to use illicit drugs more frequently than women working off-street. Our research, however, reveals a very different profile of drug and

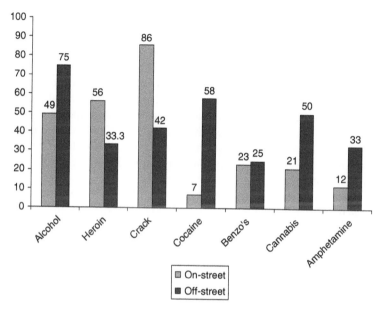

Figure 4.1 Self-reported drug and alcohol use among exited women during their involvement in prostitution (n=55)

alcohol use amongst these two groups, and suggests that illicit drug use is much more common amongst those working indoors than Jeal and Salisbury, as well as others, have suggested.

As Figure 4.1 indicates, cocaine, cannabis, alcohol and amphetamine use was much higher among women who had exited off-street prostitution than those who had exited on-street prostitution, with 50 per cent or more women involved in off-street prostitution reporting the use of cannabis and cocaine.

These findings suggest that drug taking is very prevalent amongst both groups but that the patterns of consumption are significantly different. The type of drug use that women working on-street tend to engage in is often defined as 'problematic', while the forms of consumption engaged in by those working indoors tend to be downplayed. This raises the issue of what exactly defines certain forms of drug use as 'problematic'.

According to DrugScope (2012), what makes drug use problematic is not necessarily the frequency of drug use but the effects that drug taking has on the user's life; that is, the effects that drug use has on their social, financial, psychological, physical or legal situation. The European Monitoring Centre for Drugs and Drug Addiction (EMCDDA 2008), in contrast, defines problematic drug use as: 'injecting drug use or long-duration/regular use of opiates, cocaine and/or amphetamines'. Thus, according to this definition, only certain forms of drug use qualify as 'problematic', and it is interesting that they include amphetamine and cocaine in their list. Whereas one authority claims that it is not a question of frequency but the effects of drug use, the other group suggests that it is a question of frequency and intensity of usage.

The various and competing definitions of 'problematic' drug use have been highlighted by Cave et al. (2009) in a study commissioned by the National Audit Office. These authors note the ambiguities and inconsistencies amongst the various definitions of 'problematic drug use':

> This is important because drug use may be conceived as problematic in different ways, for different reasons, by different research disciplines, government departments, agencies and practitioners. It is not surprising, therefore, that the term 'problem drug use' has been used to describe a range of different drug use behaviours in the scientific, treatment, criminal justice and other policy literatures. The definitions frequently differ around key issues, including inclusion or exclusion of particular drugs (e.g. cannabis, methamphetamines), different classifications of types of drug use (injection drug use only, dependent use) and different views about cut-off points for 'problematic' frequency of drug use (daily, weekly, etc).
>
> (Cave et al. 2009)

This statement suggests that while injecting drugs might commonly be seen and defined as 'problematic' drug use, it may from another perspective, such as the frequency and intensity of usage, be much less problematic than snorting powdered cocaine or smoking cannabis. By only defining the type of drug use engaged in by women working on-street as 'problematic', there is by implication a tendency to treat the forms of drug taking by women engaged in off-street prostitution as largely 'unproblematic'. Thus, although we know that consuming large amounts of alcohol over a long period of time can be more damaging physiologically and even socially than taking amphetamines or cannabis, for example, for many researchers this form of drug use is not seen as 'problematic', mainly because alcohol consumption is not illegal (Kalant 2010; Nutt et al. 2010). For our purposes drug use is 'problematic' in as much as it acts as a barrier to exiting, and creates a form of dependency or addiction that makes it difficult for the person to envisage change or accept help.

For 'problematic' intravenous heroin users, the preferred mode of treatment since the 1970s has been the use of methadone. This has been widely hailed as an effective treatment, which is able to sta- bilise or cure heroin addiction. However, methadone maintenance is not without its critics: it is argued by some that it simply replaces one form of addiction with another. Bourgois and Schonberg (2009), for example, argue that the birth of the methadone clinic created 'an expensive conflictive and humiliating apparatus of governmentality for regulating heroin addicts'. There are also debates and uncertain- ties about maintenance versus reduction (Gossop et al. 2001). It is claimed by some critics that methadone is far more pharmacologi- cally addictive than heroin, and that its withdrawal symptoms are notably more severe and prolonged than those caused by heroin.

However, what was perhaps most striking from the research was the proportion of women who had been involved in off-street pros- titution who reported regular use of powdered cocaine, cannabis and amphetamines during their involvement in prostitution. While these women may not identify themselves or indeed be considered by treat- ment agencies as problematic drug users, the findings clearly contra- dict the results of other research that suggest that women involved in off-street prostitution are rarely involved in illicit drug use (Cusick et al. 2003; May and Hunter 2006). Moreover, purely quantitative studies of drug use such as cross-sectional surveys of street-based and parlour-based prostitutes are unable to provide detailed information about the contexts and meanings of women's substance use, and the ways in which their use of different substances changes over time.

Women involved in off-street prostitution reported using drugs and alcohol for three main reasons – personal or recreational use; as a normalised feature of the off-street prostitution environment; and as palliative or strategy for emotional management. In their accounts of their drug and alcohol use these reasons often overlapped or merged into one another over the period of time that they were involved in prostitution. Thus, a number of women involved off-street prostitution described their use of drugs as a normal component of their lifestyle. Women in the study, particularly escorts, reported being encouraged to use drugs, especially powdered cocaine, when with clients or when socialising in mixed groups at arranged 'parties'. Some women working in brothels also reported that they had been supplied drugs (normally cocaine) by their management. While it could be argued that these patterns of recreational drug use present a low risk of harm, our interviews identified a number of women for whom this type of drug use had become intrinsically bound up with their involvement in prostitution.

While some women involved in off-street prostitution were able to seek assistance with their drug use, for some it became 'problematic' and led to a significant decline in their personal circumstances, and consequently operated as a barrier to exiting.

It is often assumed that women involved in street prostitution enter and remain in prostitution because of their addictions. However, the complexity of the relationship between drugs and prostitution is rarely addressed, and the result is that drug treatment is frequently seen as a panacea and an immediate solution to women's involvement in prostitution. However, in contrast to this simplistic model the more nuanced research on drug use and prostitution suggests that there is a more complex relationship. Potterat et al. (1998), for example, pointed out that drug use is frequently exacerbated by involvement in prostitution, while James (1976) found women who used drugs before involvement in prostitution also became heavier users after becoming involved. Young et al. (2000) and Weeks et al. (1998) have explored the ways in which drugs are used by women in prostitution as a general coping mechanism and as a response to feelings of stigma and shame. The research carried out by Young et al. (2000), for instance, points to the use of crack cocaine among women selling sex as a technique for emotional management – to mitigate the feelings of guilt and distress on one hand and as a way of increasing feelings of control and confidence on the other. Gossop et al. (2001) also found that women involved in prostitution in South London reported using heroin and alcohol in order to detach from the stresses and emotional impacts of their activities, while other studies of on-street prostitution have frequently found that drugs and alcohol are used by women in order to feel more confident, more relaxed and sociable and to suppress negative feelings (Silbert et al. 1983).

As one woman in our sample who was involved in escorting explained, her concerns about her increasing use of cocaine led her to consider exiting:

> I suppose I began noticing more and more cocaine abuse and that your days revolve around thinking about that [drugs] to get you through it. You justify like; 'Oh, I've got a three hour appointment this evening I deserve to get a gram in' and then you think why am I doing that? You know it's just to cope with the person there.

Over the last 30 years, significant amounts of funding have been directed at addressing drug use by those involved in on-street prostitution as an attempt to tackle drug-related crime (May et al. 1999). As a result, women involved in prostitution can find themselves reliant on a structure of support designed primarily to address what is defined as 'problematic' drug use, which often means intravenous drug users. Women involved in on-street prostitution may therefore appear to be better served by drug treatment support. However, this can mean that there is an over-reliance on drug treatment as a focus for exiting for this group and a lack of suitable and accessible services for women involved in off-street prostitution. Indeed, there are a number of drug treatment agencies that do not provide services for women addicted to cocaine and/or cannabis. Moreover, some women that we interviewed who were involved in on-street prostitution reported problems of accessing services that operated with rigid criteria, such as refusing treatment to women who failed to keep appointments. For the more chaotic and disorganised women, criteria of this type provided a significant obstacle to accessing treatment. Other women, particularly single mothers, reported a reluctance to visit clinics with their children or reveal that they were involved in prostitution, because they feared that their children might be taken into care.

Physical and mental health

Numerous studies have addressed the role of physical and mental health problems experienced by women involved in prostitution, while the relationship between mental health problems and other barriers has also been identified (Farley, 2004). Mental health problems such as anxiety and depression were frequently reported among women in the study who were involved in both on- and off-street prostitution as well as those trafficked into prostitution. For all three groups the combination of physical and mental health issues served as a considerable obstacle to leaving prostitution and operated as a barrier to achieve change.

When asked about their current physical and mental health, women involved in off-street prostitution reported a wide range of concerns. These women were generally more aware of and more concerned about their general physical health and readily discussed a range of health issues with researchers, including, for example, being menopausal, having polycystic ovary syndrome, an abnormal smear or high blood pressure. Some reported smoking and overeating as current health concerns.

Although generally more aware of their physical health, a number of women involved in off-street prostitution also reported some very serious and at times debilitating physical health problems, including problems with mobility (three women reported suffering arthritis), diabetes, heart attacks and liver problems caused by drug and alcohol abuse. Several women in the sample reported experiencing mental health issues including depression, panic attacks, anxiety and stress.

Women involved in on-street prostitution also experienced a wide range of physical and mental health issues. Women's health concerns within this group were generally much more complicated and connected, were often more serious and much more likely to affect other aspects of their lives.

A number of women reported problems connected to their drug addictions. Some described the addiction itself as the problem while others recognised the interrelatedness of their issues, reporting liver problems or illnesses that were associated with not eating regularly and using drugs and alcohol excessively. One woman in this group also described using drugs and alcohol as a way of managing ongoing problems with unspecific pain in her lower limbs.

Women involved in on-street prostitution also reported a wide range of serious general health concerns, including slipped disks, asthma, arthritis, high blood pressure, strokes and irritable bowel syndrome. Women in this group were less likely to discuss general health and gynaecological issues. Women involved in on-street prostitution also reported concern about their teeth, either having had teeth removed or having false teeth. This was not something reported by women involved in off-street prostitution and is suggestive of longer-term and underlying health issues among this group. The mental health issues of women involved on-street were also more complex and often more serious. Women in this group also reported depression, anxiety and panic attacks.

Money and lifestyle

As noted above, money was found to be an important barrier for many women involved in prostitution. Some had incurred debts which prevented them leaving prostitution, while for others having a disposable income and related lifestyle had become difficult to give up. Fifty-nine women (52 per cent) involved in the research reported debts, owing money to drug dealers, mortgage lenders, loan sharks, credit card and utility companies as well to housing associations and landlords. In addition, there were debts run up by coercive partners or associates under women's names.

In our sample we found, surprisingly, that a larger percentage of the off-street group (66 per cent) reported debts compared with the on-street group (49 per cent). The level of debt was also found to be higher amongst the off-street group.

Many women, particularly younger women involved in street prostitution, who were under the control of partners or pimps saw very little of the money that they earned. For example, one woman who had an abusive male partner stated:

> He used to get out of his car and say everything was going to be all right, and he would be earning money for different things . . . . Sometimes I'd have to do things that would make me violently sick. All of them in different kinds of weathers and having no sleep and having no money. It was horrible. I used to make so much money and I didn't get none of it.

Although a number of women said that they made a considerable amount of money, very few seemed to be able to hold on to it. For those engaged in heavy or expensive drug use, a great deal of their earnings were used up in this way. For others the money went to pimps, boyfriends, or was spent on 'luxury' goods and services.

Making large amounts of money in a relatively short time was seen by some women as difficult to give up, with escorts being particularly likely to use disposable cash to maintain a lifestyle to which they had become accustomed. For example, 5 of the 12 women interviewed who were involved in escorting said that despite wishing to exit they could not envisage living on a significantly reduced income:

> I was doing it for the money. So it was never like I actually wanted it. I've always been looking for something that's sensible that earns good money ... but because of the commitment financially I got, I wouldn't be able to go and work in an office now.

For some women the money that they earned through prostitution had become tarnished, and a number described it as 'dirty money' that had a value different to money made in other ways. Several women reported that as a result they were likely to 'squander' the money they had earned. Women often described earning money quickly but spending it 'impulsively' or 'recklessly'.

Violence

It is often claimed or assumed that women involved in off-street prostitution experience minimal levels of violence. However, as Raphael and Shapiro (2004) point out in their Chicago-based study of 222 women working indoors and outdoors that both groups experienced violence, although it differed in form, frequency and intensity. They found that while women working outdoors generally reported higher levels of physical violence, women working indoors were frequently victims of sexual violence. Significantly, they found that half of the women in escort services reported forced sex, with one in five of these women reporting that they had been raped more than ten times, while a third of women exchanging sexual services for money in their own premises experienced at least one form of sexual violence. Although buyers were identified as the main perpetuators of violence, one in four violent incidents amongst this sample was perpetrated by partners or pimps. They conclude from their study that the depiction of the indoor sex trade as harmless and purely consensual is mistaken.

Similarly, a comparative study carried out in the UK with 115 women involved in outdoor prostitution and 125 indoors found that 81 per cent of the women involved in street prostitution reported violence from buyers, as did almost half (48 per cent) of those working indoors. Thus although the percentage of women experiencing physical violence was considerably greater amongst those engaged in street prostitution, the percentage of those working indoors was not insignificant (Church et al. 2001). Moreover, while women outdoors more frequently reported being slapped, punched or kicked, those indoors cited attempted rape more frequently. A further study by Benoit and Miller (2001) of women engaged in off-street prostitution found that 67 per cent of respondents said that they had at one time or another received treatment for a physical injury, while 36 per cent said that they had been hospitalised specifically for injuries they had incurred while involved in the sex industry.

The women in our sample similarly reported high levels of violence, with 86 per cent of the entire sample experiencing some form of violence while involved in prostitution. Experiences of violence differed significantly between groups, with 90 per cent of women involved in on-street prostitution compared with 75 per cent of women involved indoors reporting experiences of violence while involved in selling sex. The main difference between groups was violence from a buyer, which was reported by 80 per cent of women in the on-street sample and 50 per cent of women in the off-street sample. Women involved on-street were also much more likely to report experiencing physical and sexual violence from punters than those off-street – 70 per cent compared with 31 per cent experienced physical violence and 53 per cent compared with 21 per cent experienced sexual violence. Women off-street, however, were more likely to report intimidation and verbal abuse from buyers, with nearly a third (31 per cent) reporting this form of violence compared with 17 per cent of women involved on street.

Women involved in prostitution also experienced significant violence at the hands of their pimps, with 46 per cent of women involved on-street compared with 25 per cent of women involved off-street reporting it. Violence perpetrated by pimps was more commonly physical or emotional in nature rather than sexual, with relatively few women (6 per cent) involved in on-street or off-street prostitution reporting this type of violence.

However, those engaged in off-street prostitution pointed out the dangers associated with being in a closed or sometimes locked room with 'dodgy' buyers, and claimed that if you are working outdoors at least you have a chance of running away if you feel threatened. The level and degree of different kinds of violence experienced by women involved in prostitution obviously varies according to the setting and the context in which the sexual transaction takes place; but the frequency and intensity of violence in all sectors suggests that it is unlikely to be reduced through 'ugly mugs' campaigns (which may inadvertently create a false sense of security) or to be designed out through the use of environmental measures (Sanders and Campbell 2007). Like domestic violence and other activities that occur behind closed doors, environmental controls are just as likely to 'design in' as 'design out' violence. Moreover, the level of violence reported by those engaged in on-street and off-street prostitution strongly suggests that violence is endemic in the sex industry and is not just a problem created by a few exceptional buyers (Wahab 2005); and as we have seen in the case of the Netherlands, violence, threats and abuse are unlikely to be reduced through legalisation (Raymond 2013).

The experience of violence can affect women involved in prostitution in different ways. On one hand the exposure to serious and consistent violence can prompt some women to consider exiting, while on the other the exercise of violence from pimps and partners and managers can prevent or deter women who want to get out of prostitution from leaving. Thus the violence can be both an incentive and a disincentive to exiting, and consideration needs to be given to the form of violence experienced and the nature and objectives of the perpetrators of violence.

Criminalisation

In most cases criminalisation serves as a barrier to exiting. Gaining a criminal record and therefore becoming more marginalised also tends to increase vulnerability and victimisation. In a limited number of cases, however, engagement with the criminal justice system can provide women with the motivation to exit. Moreover, as we have seen in the previous chapter, women involved in prostitution tend to have histories of a range of criminal involvement; but there are significant differences between the two groups.

Thirty-seven per cent of the on-street group had convictions for drug-related offences, 36 per cent for offences against the person and 70 per cent for acquisitive crime. This compares with 21 per cent, 12 per cent and 30 per cent, respectively, for women involved in off-street prostitution. What is significant about these findings is that the number of convictions for acquisitive crime is virtually double that of the other two crime categories. Previous research has identified the link between involvement in acquisitive crime and drug dependency (Gossop et al. 2006).

Having a conviction of any type is likely to serve as an obstacle to exiting and to finding legitimate employment. Specialist agencies, however, exist to help those with convictions to find employment. At present there is not a great deal of emphasis amongst support agencies to link up with specialist employment agencies, and more could be done to find these women work. A significant number have different skills and experience, but may require training in order to find suitable work.

Turning points and support

Specific incidents that were associated with the decision to exit were similar in many respects for both groups, and included finding new relationships and becoming pregnant. Other studies have also identified the importance of relationships in the process of women's desistance, and finding a new partner or becoming pregnant appears to be an important turning point for a number of women (McIvor et al. 2004).

In our analysis of exiting, we have referred to a group of women who left prostitution with minimal support as 'self exiters'. Amongst the sample of women who had exited, the data suggest that this is more common among women involved in off-street rather than on-street prostitution. There seemed to be a number of factors associated with self-exiting: these include maturation, pregnancy, social capital, having a limited number of barriers to overcome and some degree of informal support.

Some women simply reported that they felt they had been involved in prostitution long enough, and that they were getting older and presumably finding it more difficult to make enough money. Pregnancy was an important factor for both groups, and many of these women felt that having a baby and bringing up a child was incompatible with prostitution. Relatedly, finding a new partner was also seen as a reason to break with prostitution, and some women pointed out that they thought that developing this new relationship necessitated leaving prostitution. These new relationships did not necessarily involve marriage but rather a greater commitment to one person and the formation of a steady relationship. Underpinning the decision to move amongst the women involved in off-street prostitution was greater confidence in their ability to find alternative forms of income and support. For women in the on-street group the experience of serious violence or their involvement in the criminal justice system, as well as forming new relationships or becoming pregnant, provided the motivation for them to exit.

There were found to be significant differences between the role of formal and informal support accessed by both groups of women. Significantly, for the on-street group formal support in the form of drug treatment and housing provision played a critical role in ten cases, while this was only the main factor in exiting for three women involved in indoor prostitution.

Identity formation and social structure

We have noted above that many women involved in prostitution are able to block off past experiences in order to maintain a sense of self-identity. In addition, the issue of identity plays another key role in relation to exiting. This supplementary role refers to the extent to which women identify themselves as 'prostitutes'. Not all people who sell sex identify themselves as 'prostitutes' or 'sex workers', and much depends on the level and nature of involvement in the sex trade.

The sex industry is highly segmented, and there are significant differences in the modus operandi of women located on the street, in brothels, private flats and those acting as escorts (Weitzer 2005). These different contexts will affect women's experiences, conditions, ability to refuse buyers, victimisation and the degree of control to which they are subject. These situational and social factors will, in turn, influence their sense of self-identity.

Research on male prostitution has drawn attention to the differential involvement of people in the sex trade, and that some young men selling sex may not define themselves either as homosexual or as prostitutes (Boyer 1989). These studies raise issues about the levels of commitment to selling sex, the degree of immersion in the sex trade and the extent to which individuals take on a prostitute identity.

This issue also arises in relation to the runaways and homeless people who engage in so-called 'survival sex'. Although this group falls within the general definition of prostitution, by 'providing sexual services for money or payment', in many cases they may not identify themselves as prostitutes. In 2004 it was estimated that some 5,000 children and young people were involved in prostitution in the UK, and that many are runaways, homeless or have been in local authority care (Levy 2004). In the United States it is estimated that several hundred thousand young runaways engage in selling sex in some form each year (Flowers 2001). For many the selling of sex is instrumental, and in cases in which their involvement is relatively short term they are unlikely to take on a prostitute identity.

In contrast, there were some women whom we interviewed who found exiting difficult because they had fully internalised a prostitute identity. For example, one woman who was trying to exit said:

> I was really struggling with having this huge identity crisis. Like I was not going out, selling sex. I wasn't using drugs. I wasn't employed and I wasn't doing a legit job.... But I kind of figured that if I wasn't a prostitute I really don't know who I am. I didn't have no idea who I was. And I didn't see how that would ever change because it feels like it is so deep rooted.

What is important about observations such as this is that there is a difference between selling sex and identifying oneself as a prostitute on one hand and the effects of different degrees of immersion in the sex trade on the other. It seems probable that for those who do not take on a prostitute identity exiting may be much easier, while those whose involvement is sporadic are also likely to find it easier to leave prostitution. These are important considerations when thinking about developing practices that relate to exiting, and provide a corrective against treating all those involved in selling sex as a homogeneous group. Therefore, when assessments are being made about different individuals, these issues of identity and the type of involvement in the sex trade need to be taken into account (O'Neill 2001).

Paradoxically, women in our sample involved on-street were more likely to identify more fully with the 'prostitute' identity than women involved off-street. Women working off-street tended to be able to compartmentalise their involvement in prostitution and had other facets of their identity that they could draw on. Off-street women often chose to exit when they began to feel that they were no longer able to manage these multiple roles, or when their core identity began to feel contaminated by their involvement in prostitution. However, those women whose involvement in prostitution is more structured because they are located in brothels may feel a greater level of constraint than those who are involved in street prostitution, who are able to engage in the sex trade in a more flexible manner. These different experiences, constraints and motivations mean that the support required to exit needs to have a different orientation for the two groups.

For women who have been trafficked, the issue of a prostitute identity is even more problematic. For the migrant women in the UK who have been forced, deceived, threatened or have become involved in the sex trade through debt bondage, most are more likely to identify themselves as victims rather than 'prostitutes'.

Trafficked women

The process of exiting does not strictly apply to trafficked women. While trafficked women are commercially sexually exploited, often within off-street locations, it is uncommon for these women to view themselves as choosing their circumstances; indeed, the majority of these women view themselves as being subjected to repeated rape. Even women with a history of involvement in prostitution before being trafficked rarely identify themselves as exiting prostitution but rather as 'escaping' or being recovered from commercial sexual exploitation. It was clear from the trafficked women in our sample that recovering from their experiences of being trafficked into the sex trade was far from a straightforward process, and that once they had managed to get out of prostitution they faced similar problems to other groups of women who were trying to exit.

However, as the Anti-Trafficking Monitoring Group (2010) has pointed out, there is considerable uncertainty in relation to the identification of 'trafficked' persons and the operation of the key referral agencies that have been set up to respond to those who have been trafficked. The combination of these two issues has had serious implications in the UK regarding who qualifies as a 'trafficked' person and what type of services they receive. It is argued by the Anti-Trafficking Monitoring Group that the current system relies on the discretion of officials who receive minimal training and who are reliant on flawed legal guidance regarding who should be identified as victims of trafficking. At the same time, the system appears to be putting more emphasis on the immigration status of the presumed trafficked persons rather than dealing with the alleged crime committed against them. It is also reported that a significant number of people who have been trafficked do not have their cases reported to support organisations, either because they did not see any benefit in being referred or were fearful of the consequences. Thus:

> When victims are wrongly identified this has serious consequences for the person concerned: it risks compounding the already traumatic experience of having been trafficked by setting back their recovery and removing any faith individuals may have had in the authorities and their ability to offer protection and assistance thus undermining prosecutions and causing further breaches of individuals' human rights.
>
> (Anti-Trafficking Monitoring Group 2010: 10)

An example of the limited application of the definition of 'trafficking' is evident in a recent report by the Association of Chief Police Officers (Jackson et al. 2010). This report claims that there were approximately 17,000 migrant women involved in off-street prostitution in the UK in 2010. Of these, 2,600 were defined as being trafficked. These people qualified as 'trafficked persons' on the basis that they were highly vulnerable, subject to coercion, threats or some form of debt bondage. However, they also identify a second group of 9,600 people:

> Although they have elements of vulnerability to trafficking most are likely to fall short of the trafficking threshold. There may be cultural or financial factors which prevent them from exiting prostitution (or seeking help to do so) but they tend to have day to day control over their activities, and although they may

have large debts they generally do not consider themselves to be debt-bonded.

(Jackson et al. 2010: 5)

However, according to Article 4 of the Council of Europe Convention Against Trafficking in Human Beings, which was ratified by the UK in 2008, the definition of trafficking means the 'recruitment, transportation, transfer, harbouring or receipt of persons, by means of threat or use of force or other forms of coercion, of abduction, of fraud, or deception, of the abuse of power or of a position of vulnerability'. In addition, it states that the definition of trafficking includes 'the exploitation of prostitution of others or other forms of sexual exploitation'.

It is difficult to believe that many of the second group of the 9,600 who are identified as vulnerable and have identifiable barriers to exiting do not meet the Council of Europe's definition of trafficking. Because they are not defined as victims of trafficking, the implication is that they are unlikely to access the appropriate support services and may be interrogated, detained or deported (Kelly 2003).

Even among identified victims access to services is usually patchy. Dedicated accommodation for trafficked women is in theory available in the UK. In practice, however, space in appropriate accommodation is not always available. As with many involved in on-street prostitution the need for secure accommodation is of paramount importance, in order to provide a base from which to reorganise their lives. In addition many trafficked women are often the victims of coercion or deception, and like many women involved in prostitution there is a problem of trust and self-esteem. As one trafficked women stated:

> I just feel that it was all my fault. It's me who feels guilty because I think if I wasn't so trusting it would not have happened. On the other hand I say to myself I have to trust somebody. I can't live without trusting anybody.

Apart from trying to re-establish trust, trafficked women often require support with language and translation when accessing legal advice regarding immigration issues. Women who were interviewed expressed deep reservations about contacting the police and providing information on traffickers because of fears of reprisals.

Women also spoke about fears that they would be ostracised if their families found out that they had been involved in the sex trade. Limited education in some cases and limited language skills mean that women who have 'escaped' find it difficult to find legitimate forms of training or employment, and there is the likelihood of re-engagement in the sex trade either in the UK or when they return to their own country.

Trafficked women tend not to take on a prostitute identity, seeing themselves quite rightly as victims of coercion and deception. Consequently they are more effectively able to neutralise their involvement in prostitution. Although this should be an important factor in their efforts to 'exit', the other barriers that they face mean that it is often very difficult to readjust to normal life.

In terms of strategy, therefore, a number of measures need to be developed in order to help trafficked women move on. According to the practitioners involved in the study, women trafficked into commercial sexual exploitation require immediate support in relation to entering the formal National Referral Mechanism (NRM) process and in relation to their immigration status. In the early stages women also often require access to health care, safe accommodation and psychological and emotional support, and women opting to engage in proceedings against traffickers frequently need support to provide evidence before and during legal proceedings. The United Kingdom's adherence to the United Nations Convention dictates to a certain extent the types of support available to women who have been formally identified as trafficked within the NRM or who are currently going through the NRM process. As a result these women can become involved in the complicated networks that exist between statutory services, such as the border agency, police and prosecutors, and the services commissioned by government and in the voluntary sector that provide a range of support to victims.

Women involved in prostitution who do not fall under the provisions of the Convention (including women who do not agree to referral into the NRM) are not provided with any statutory provision as 'victims'. In England and Wales, support for women within the NRM process and those who are formally identified as trafficked is provided by the Salvation Army under contract to central government. Some of this support is then subcontracted, and is therefore dependent upon local configuration of services and capacity.

Where exiting support is provided to those whose circumstances fall outside the requirements of the Convention, such support tends to operate over a longer period and in a more fluid and less structured way than that provided through the centralised framework to those identified as victims or possible victims of trafficking. Good exiting support for these women focuses on the key-work relationship, building self-esteem and confidence, long-term counselling, and on addressing key barriers to exit, such as drug treatment; education, training and employment; and on creating a viable alternative identity and lifestyle.

A small proportion of women who are recovered from their trafficking situation return to their involvement in prostitution. One woman in our sample who had become addicted to crack cocaine returned to prostitution after having been freed from the clutches of traffickers. This group often includes women who have limited resources and few alternatives, women who have residence permits but with no recourse to public funds. This group of women is likely to benefit from the support of exiting services designed to address the needs of women involved in indoor prostitution; however, it is uncommon for funding to be provided for these groups even where established exiting programmes exist.

The normal forms of exiting support are therefore not a substitute for targeted, resourced intervention for women who experience human trafficking for the purposes of commercial sexual exploitation. The complex issues that accompany human trafficking, both for victims and for services addressing this issue mean that independent specialist exiting and human trafficking services are required. While there are some overlaps between the two groups, support for trafficking victims is generally made available under a formal framework. However, in cases in which women are not formally identified as victims of trafficking, or where their status is unclear, access to well-resourced exiting provision will be important.

Conclusion

The main differences between the two groups were that a greater proportion of on-street women experienced barriers to exiting, particularly in relation to drug use, housing, having a criminal record and lack of qualifications. However, both groups reported high levels of drug use and physical and mental problems, while more of the off-street women said that they had financial problems and debts.

Rebuilding trust was found to be an important part of the exiting process for these women, many of whom had suffered years of abuse and neglect, while maturation seemed to play a more important role amongst the women involved in off-street prostitution, with a higher proportion of self-exiters in this group. For those involved in off-street prostitution exiting involved overcoming identity crises and peer pressure. Becoming pregnant was an important factor for both groups, and the prospect of having a child and fears about it being taken into care prompted many women to consider exiting.

Women involved in on-street prostitution were found to experience much higher levels of physical and sexual violence, including threats and rape. These experiences can have different effects on different women in different contexts. In some cases they serve to maintain them in prostitution through fear and dependency, while in others they can act as catalysts for change.

Debt and various financial problems were reported to be experienced by members of both groups, but this was surprisingly prevalent amongst women involved in off-street prostitution. For some their continued involvement in prostitution was seen as the best way to pay off debts, while others recognised that they were able to save little or none of the money that they earned, and therefore decided that the only way to break with this vicious circle was to exit.

The women who had been trafficked seldom 'exited' in the same way as other women involved in prostitution. Indeed, the terms 'exiting' and 'desistance' hardly apply to many of these women. Instead, we can talk in terms of them escaping, or in some cases being rescued. However, whether they escape or are rescued the break with prostitution is in most cases not straightforward or clear-cut. Many experience different forms of trauma and distress and find it very difficult to move on. Others have in the course of their involvement in prostitution come to take on a prostitute identity, and experience a temptation to continue their involvement in prostitution in some form. Others become more heavily involved in drug and alcohol consumption in order to block out past experiences. For these reasons, women who have been trafficked require specialist care in order to recover from their ordeal. Unfortunately, in a significant number of cases the authorities either do not define these women as legitimate 'victims' or only support the women while they are giving evidence against traffickers, or alternatively deport them.

A great deal of the focus in recent years has been on women involved in on-street prostitution, particularly the more damaged and chaotic individuals. However, there are many women involved in off-street prostitution who are interested in exiting but find it difficult to access appropriate support. Many of these women are isolated and marginalised, and unlikely to make use of drop-in centres and established prostitution support agencies. Although the majority of women involved in indoor prostitution are not intravenous drug users and not addicted to crack cocaine, many do consume considerable quantities of drugs and have different kinds of addiction. If a more comprehensive exiting service is to be established, therefore, greater contact needs to be made with women involved in off-street prostitution, and the response of the relevant agencies requires adjustment if they are to accommodate their needs and aspirations.

5
Models of Service Provision

Introduction

Support and treatment agencies can play a critical role in the exiting process. In the course of our research, we examined various forms of service provision and assessed their respective contributions to exiting. These agencies, we found, have different philosophies, objectives and practice. Thus the central focus of this chapter is how women involved in different types of prostitution utilise support services, and how the different forms of service provision are able to contribute to the exiting process.

Amongst the services provided for the women in our sample, it was clear that their ethos and approaches to prostitution and exiting varied widely. Some agencies saw exiting as peripheral to the service that they provided, while others had a clear commitment to promoting exiting as an important goal in itself. Close examination of the data, however, indicated that each of the services could be broadly categorised in relation to the type of exiting support provided. Although there was some variation within each category, a typology of four models emerged: (a) harm minimisation plus; (b) women's service/women's centre; (c) multi-agency partnerships; and (d) a case management approach.

A number of factors influenced how different agencies provided a service, including, for example, the nature of the organisation providing the service; the size of the team; the political context within which the service operates; the provision by other related agencies; the effectiveness of local strategic partnerships; and the level of communication and cooperation between key agencies. It is also important to note that services providing exiting support for women are frequently dynamic, responding to changes in the identified needs of service users; funding availability; commissioning processes; and shifting local, regional and national government priorities. A service may therefore develop and move from one category of the typology to another over time. For the purposes of this analysis, however, each service has been categorised according to its characteristics at the time of the original research. Services and provision also varied somewhat within categories, and such variations are explored in more detail in the subsections below.

Harm minimisation plus

Services in the harm minimisation plus category have developed from harm reduction or health promotion initiatives. Such services have historically targeted key populations with the aim of reducing the short-term but serious consequences of high-risk activities, such as the transmission of blood-borne viruses through injecting drug use (Velleman and Rigby 1990).

According to Riley et al. (1999), harm reduction principles are value neutral, pragmatic and concerned with prioritising achievable goals. Harm minimisation therefore adopts the view that drug use and prostitution are here to stay, and that the focus should be on reducing harm rather than attempting to change behaviour. In relation to prostitution, harm minimisation organisations are usually involved in the provision of outreach or drop-in services, where women involved in on-street prostitution can receive support for their immediate needs. Typically this includes the provision of a warm drink, clean clothes, access to toiletries and shower facilities, free condoms, sexual health testing, needle exchange services, advice about safer sexual or injecting practices, and the availability of someone to talk to. Women may also be supported to report incidents of sexual violence, and projects such as these are often first points of contact for women interested in taking up other support services or in exiting prostitution.

Harm minimisation approaches assume that those engaging in risky and harmful behaviours such as drug use and prostitution are 'rational' people able to make a choice about their lifestyle. They tend to focus on minimising immediate harms, and typically adopt a reactive approach to exiting by responding to requests for support to leave prostitution. In cases where women actively seek help and support to leave prostitution, these harm minimisation agencies will normally formulate a strategy in conjunction with the women concerned, initially focusing on resolving problems with substance misuse or unsuitable accommodation.

While such services frequently come into contact with women who identify and vocalise their desire to exit prostitution, historically this support has been offered on a sporadic basis only when women claim that they are ready to leave. Indeed, some supporters of this approach argue that proactively engaging women and directly offering them exiting support is an 'affront to human dignity' (Cusick et al. 2011).

The exiting support available through the harm minimisation model is generally focused on the needs expressed by individual women rather than an underlying exiting strategy or theory. In this context, exiting support has usually been informal and reliant on the contacts and capacities of individual workers rather than operating through formal and established relationships. As an outreach worker from Turning Point explained when asked which model of exiting they employed replied:

> Oh Lord, I don't like being asked theoretical questions 'cos I always feel like I should know them. What model? Well, I meet them, see what they need to do, what they want support with and then we do it.

Increasingly, however, some harm minimisation agencies have begun to provide more structured support for women exiting prostitution, usually through the provision of a dedicated support worker as an 'add on' to core provision. It is this approach that is referred to throughout this chapter as 'harm minimisation plus'. Some commentators argue that the recent growth in exiting specific posts is the result of changes to government strategy and policy on prostitution, with services being required to include 'exiting' in order to maintain a suitable level of funding (Cusick et al. 2011). Examples of services offering this type of provision are Turning Point in Sheffield and the GAP Project in Newcastle. In East London a number of women were referred to Safe Exit from Compass Isis, a specialist women's service providing support to substance-misusing women, many of whom are involved in prostitution.

Perhaps the most fully developed exiting support available through a harm minimisation agency was the work of the support and options worker at Genesis. While not openly labelled as an 'exiting' worker, this role delivers case-managed one-to-one support for women to 'move on' and make 'positive changes' in their lives. The support and options worker undertakes risk assessments, support plans and referral assessments for each woman, with a focus on moving women on from their involvement in prostitution. As well as providing support for women involved in on-street prostitution, the worker also has a role in raising awareness of exiting among women working in flats and saunas. At the time of the interviews, this was a new post created to formalise and extend exiting work that was part of the 'holistic' support provided by Genesis for many years. Interviews with support workers from the GAP Project in Newcastle indicated that individual one-to-one support for women with complex needs was a relatively new form of provision, and something which they were working to develop.

The stakeholders interviewed felt that delivering exiting support within a harm minimisation context had a number of benefits for women. First, and perhaps most importantly, interviewees felt that adopting this approach meant the service could build trust with women and then allow them to move on to one-to-one support when and if they identified this as something they would like. Interviewees also felt that services providing this type of support were non-judgemental, and were responsive to the needs women had identified for themselves rather than imposing a view that women should be encouraged to exit. Several of the services providing this type of exiting support have been proactive in engaging with women in saunas, brothels and flats as well as women operating independently as escorts.

There are, however, a number of limitations of this approach. First, there is a tendency to focus largely on practical support, for example referrals into prescribing services; assistance with housing or accessing benefits; or support attending court or meetings with statutory services. While this approach generally supports women who voice a desire to leave prostitution, or may suggest women exit prostitution when their lives are in crisis, it does not often proactively address exiting as an option and may therefore fail to generate sufficient opportunities for women to openly consider the pros and cons of their involvement in prostitution. Maintaining such a service user-led ethos may mean that women continue to engage in behaviour which causes them significant harm without considering the long-term and cumulative effects of such behaviour. Such an approach also may not actively engage with women's feelings of ambivalence or shame; identify or engage effectively with the dynamics of coercion that women have experienced in connection to their involvement in prostitution; or support women sufficiently to overcome a damaged identity or low self-esteem.

Funding of harm minimisation plus services is often tied to the realisation of designated outcomes and objectives, but as the outreach worker at Turning Point in Sheffield explained:

> They like the people to fit into little boxes don't they? They like people to travel from Tier 1 services into Tier 2, and then into Tier 3 and then into Tier 4 and then out. But it doesn't work like that. The NTA [National Treatment Agency] ask for all this information and it's not always practical. I appreciate that it's necessary and funding related but some of the things are unrealistic.

Exiting workers employed alongside harm minimisation projects, particularly those that are part of generic rather than specialist services, may find themselves operating in isolation with little opportunity to develop shared practice and professional skills in relation to exiting. The worker from Turning Point, for example, reported that she was the only person in the organisation who worked with women involved in prostitution. This reality may lead to issues where workers are left without suitable line management or where there is no exiting support for women when a worker is on leave. As the funding for such posts is also often provided from sources other than those that fund the main harm minimisation provision, conflicts of interest or differences in relation to key issues such as data protection and outcome monitoring may arise. This may further isolate workers delivering exiting support and impact on their capacity to deliver.

The women interviewed were positive about the availability of outreach and drop-in services that supported them while they continued to sell sex. For some women contact with outreach and drop-in services had been a route into exiting support, which had helped them permanently leave prostitution. For others, who were already motivated to exit, outreach and drop-in services provided an initial point of contact, which allowed them to receive support. However, many of the women that we interviewed said that despite having an awareness of such services, they had not been motivated to seek support with exiting until they had experienced serious 'turning point' or their lives had fallen into crisis.

It is clear from the research that harm minimisation services have a vital role to play in relation to women's involvement in prostitution, for without this basic support and initial point of contact, women would often not be in a position to exit. Indeed, in some cases, harm minimisation services can provide the type of services and level of support required to assist some women to leave.

However, in other cases, harm minimisation projects, rather than offering exiting as an option and empowering women to make an informed 'choice', may have the effect of maintaining women in prostitution when in fact they want to leave (Matthews 2008; Miller 2001; Roe 2005). For some of the women interviewed who were motivated to exit, this avoidance of exiting made it difficult to obtain the support they were looking for. One woman in our sample, for instance, reported feeling that she had insulted her support worker by asking for support to exit prostitution. She said:

> Yeah, and I wasn't aware, I don't think I was aware that such services existed and like there were a lot of venues, like I knew there were quite a few services that did street outreach and harm minimisation and stuff, but in terms of support actually getting out of it .... Yeah, like when I mentioned that to another agency that I had been at they were almost a bit, I don't know, he just didn't take it very well, it's almost like they were quite offended.

Others were supported by harm minimisation services with pragmatic issues, such as housing or substance misuse, but were left to flounder for many years in temporary accommodation located in 'red light' districts with no real possibility of making meaningful changes in their lives. Furthermore, adopting a pragmatic approach means that women are often encouraged to resolve their substance misuse issues in isolation from their involvement in prostitution, despite much evidence that women often use drugs in order to cope with their experiences in prostitution. This is likely to be one of the reasons for the rates of drop out from drug treatment among women involved in prostitution.

Findings from our research suggest that while many women involved in prostitution had considered exiting they did not always discuss this possibility with their key worker. The reasons cited by women for not immediately voicing a desire to exit prostitution varied. Some women, particularly those involved in street prostitution, felt unable to conceptualise a life beyond prostitution or to believe that they had sufficient strength to make such significant changes. Other women, often those making significant amounts of money in indoor prostitution or escorting, explained that their immediate peer group did not allow them to discuss their dissatisfaction or the difficulties they faced in prostitution. Such views were usually considered a failure of the individual to cope rather than a problem inherent within prostitution. Among our sample, women reported that discussions of exiting among this group generally focused on long-term, planned, strategic exits rather than immediate exits based on personal or emotional reactions to selling sex. Findings such as these suggest that women welcome the opportunity to talk about exiting, and to explore the exiting possibilities available to them and that women involved in indoor prostitution might in fact welcome opportunities to discuss exiting rather than viewing it as an 'affront'.

The harm minimisation plus model may also be unintentionally selective in relation to the women who are offered support to exit. For example, women with greater personal capacities and resources who want to and are able to exit may receive sufficient support to do so through the harm minimisation plus model, while women who cannot see a life beyond prostitution or who are less able to be assertive and discuss their desire to exit may never access such support, instead making attempts to exit on their own or through other services, such as drug rehabilitation.

A women-centred approach

In recent years there has been a growth in gender-specific provision for women, particularly with a focus on supporting women offenders or women at risk of offending. While women's centres such as these provide a range of support for women and work with women involved in prostitution, this is not their primary focus. Such services differ vastly in their approach and their sources of funding, but aim to deliver similar 'holistic' or 'one-stop shop' support for women from a range of backgrounds who present with similar underlying needs and particular vulnerabilities (Corston 2007; Radcliffe et al. 2013).

Services which fall into the women's centre/women's service model usually provide intensive, structured, therapeutic and pragmatic support from a dedicated central location. Services provide a range of targeted group work and courses as well as one-to-one case management. Many women's centres provide outreach, both in the community and with key agencies, as well as a range of in-house specialist provision, including needle exchange, housing and benefits advice, washing facilities, meals and access to training and educational opportunities. Where provision is not possible within the centre, links are made with external agencies that are capable of providing specific services, such as counselling, complementary therapies, child care, drug treatment and so on. Such services may be delivered either on or off site. Women's centres such as these generally work with a structured approach, which generally supports more vulnerable and marginalised women without a specific focus on prostitution. Such services are therefore not intended to meet the needs of women involved in street-based prostitution, and are not relevant for many other women involved in selling sex.

Two of the services involved in our research fell into this category – Women at the Well (WATW) in North London and Together Women (TW) in Leeds. WATW was established in 2008, but at the time of the study had only been operating for 18 months. The organisation is faith-based, has a multi-agency board and receives funding from the Sisters of Mercy and the Ministry of Justice. The service operates with three paid staff and approximately 25 volunteer staff, including a large number of nuns who have prior experience working as teachers or social workers. The service provides open door support for women from any background. Referrals are also taken from statutory and non-statutory organisations such as Compass Isis, the Terrence Higgins Trust, New Horizons and local outreach teams. The service provides a drop-in day service for all women and a range of coordinated activities for those who wish to attend. The service also provides evening hot meals twice a week, which staff and service users take together.

WATW estimate that approximately half of their service users are involved in street prostitution, and a quarter are considered to be entrenched in chaotic lifestyles and experiencing other issues such as homelessness and substance misuse (particularly crack and heroin). The service reports that approximately 10 per cent of women accessing the service have been issued ASBOs by the local authorities and that a number have been subject to recent arrests.

Women involved in prostitution present to the service with a variety of needs and are often in crisis, as they have just left prison, been evicted or left a crack house; are heavy users of alcohol, heroin and/or crack; have legal issues such as ASBOs or involvement in other offending; have had their children removed from their care; experience significant mental and physical health issues; or have a number of other vulnerabilities and needs.

The service aims to support women over the long term by providing support; encouraging women to discuss their needs; providing an inclusive atmosphere; arranging access to rapid scripting and drug treatment; offering assistance with form-filling and advice with benefits and housing; delivering training and workshops; arranging legal support (e.g. in relation to ASBOs); and accompanying women to key appointments. WATW views its service users as vulnerable and socially excluded women, and while it predominantly takes a harm reduction approach it also provides support for women wanting to exit prostitution.

According to the project coordinator of the service, the aim is to facilitate a woman's exit as far as possible by supporting her to overcome the barriers she encounters along the way:

> Making it as easy as possible, I think that's what we try and do here. So for instance you are taking people to appointments, you're making assessments as painless as possible because they're not things that have to happen. They're things that you need to get through this hurdle to get to that. It's just making life as easy as possible for that woman because why make it more difficult than it already is. And I think if you make things easy, if you take people to things, if you help them or do paperwork for them, if you try to get away all the obstacles you just make that transition so much

easier for them and so much, if you take away those boundaries there's less and less excuses for why things can't happen.

The TW project opened in 2007 as part of a Home Office-funded 'national demonstration project', aiming to address the needs of women offenders as identified in the Corston Report (2007). Five centres were established in the North West and Yorkshire and Humberside National Offender Management Service Regions. TW aims to provide support for women offenders and women at risk of offending; also to provide alternative sentencing strategies for women offenders and to divert women away from prison, where the harms for women offenders are well known. While the service has no specific remit for women involved in prostitution, these women are considered 'at risk' of arrest and prosecution and have similar underlying needs to women offenders.

Referrals are made from probation, social services, health, the police, courts and a range of local non-statutory services that work with women involved in prostitution. The service also accepts women who self-refer. Women's attendance is predominantly in a voluntary capacity. Some women's attendance at the centre can also count towards their probation supervision.

The five TW centres were encouraged to develop services according to local demand. The services at Leeds TW are therefore similar but not the same as services elsewhere in the region. In Leeds, women have access to one-to-one advice and support, counselling, a crèche, group programmes and so on. The centre is also used as a safe women-only space where women can, for example, meet with other agencies or have supervised access to their children. Where appropriate and possible, the service conducts home visits or supports women to access other local services. The support offered by TW is on average of four to six months in duration.

The service has no specific policy about how to work with women who are involved in prostitution; rather, all women are assessed and provided with support on the basis of their individual needs. Women attending the service are not asked to disclose their involvement in prostitution, and it was the belief of both the substance misuse support worker and centre manager that many of the women using the service were involved in prostitution but chose not to disclose this information. While service delivery was no different for women whether they disclosed involvement in prostitution or not, it was acknowledged that women involved in prostitution often had a number of needs which were not well met by TW, particularly at the early stages when women were most chaotic. As the centre manager reported, women involved in prostitution who were engaging with TW had generally moved on from a chaotic lifestyle and came to the service to engage in specific activities or interventions:

> As a general rule we work with far fewer numbers of women with chaotic lifestyles. The nature of what we do is a little more structured, and as times evolve there are more substance misuse agencies that have structured crisis intervention, outreach, night-time staff, agencies that work specifically with working women who meet that particular need. And we're maybe a little step from that, where women are, maybe not exiting but just maybe a little step on from absolute chaos and able to keep an appointment, and who might want to come in and do something every Tuesday or every Wednesday. That might be their starting point.

Both the substance misuse support worker and the centre manager felt that the TW service was not particularly able to deal with the multiple and complex needs of women involved in street prostitution. This was because, first, the service was only able to provide support over a three to six month period, which was rarely long enough to develop sufficient trust let alone to undertake the work required with this group of women. Second, the service was not sufficiently resourced to provide the support that some of these women required, for example, with serious mental health issues such as depression and self-harm, with mobility issues which were the result of deep vein thrombosis brought on from injecting drug use, and those who were unable to keep appointments owing to patterns of chaotic drug use and prostitution, controlling partners or lack of self-confidence. Women such as these often dropped out of the service and tended to be viewed as non-engagers rather than women with multiple issues, for whom the service was unable to cater. Women such as these might be re-referred to the service; however, in order to do this women face repeated questioning about their past and are generally viewed as 'problematic', thus further deterring such women from engaging. There is, therefore, a danger that while generic provision for women is available, it is unable to meet the particular needs of women involved in prostitution, many of whom are the most marginalised and most at risk.

While services in this category are usually well informed about the different needs of women, and often encounter many women involved in prostitution, the way in which they work with these women varies, and is often not a core focus of the service. While this generic approach may be viewed positively, as arguably it may minimise the stigma of involvement in prostitution and provide positive non-prostitution role models for women, it may also prevent sufficient focus on the particular needs and issues faced by women who have been selling sex. A key challenge faced by generic women's services is how to deliver support for women engaging in different behaviours, for example, combinations of offending, substance misuse and prostitution, and who may be at different stages of change or have very different levels of need. For services accepting referrals from the criminal justice system, there is the added complexity of managing work with women who attend on a voluntary basis and those who are required to attend in order to meet the needs of a conditional caution, court diversion or probation order, for instance.

Generic women's services tend to provide fragmented provision involving onward referral to multiple services with multiple key workers, assessments, physical locations and rules of engagement. Generic provision is also unable to provide specialist understanding of how issues related to physical health, drug abuse, mental health, domestic violence and coercion, and historic and contemporary sexual trauma interact and influence present behaviour.

Despite these challenges, services such as these have a number of strengths. First, they provide a women-only space, usually in a city centre location where women can access a wide range of services. They also offer structured one-to-one support and rapid links into specialist provision such as substitute prescribing, housing, legal advice and benefits advice, as well as offering other practical and emotional support. Women's services, particularly those involved with the criminal justice system, often keep detailed records about women's engagement, and have processes and policies in place in relation to measuring key outcomes, client confidentiality, data protection and information sharing. While reporting was considered in some cases to be resource intensive and time consuming, as the centre manager at TWP explained, recording client contact data is important, not only to be able to report back to funders but also, perhaps more importantly, in order to provide women with the best service possible:

> Some agencies feel you shouldn't keep records on the women, that it's, it's not okay to do that. I feel like you are not giving them a proper service unless you've got some records and that's not answering to funders, but if Sharon Smith comes in and you do a bit of a health needs assessment and you do a bit of work with her, if you don't record that then where's your starting point for next time? I think you are not doing her any, a good service, by not keeping proper records.

A review of prostitution-related services in Glasgow noted that keeping records and monitoring progress is important for three main reasons: (1) being able to effectively identify the needs of women who make multiple presentations to the service and to begin to provide services on the basis of this information; (2) the service is better able to accurately measure the nature and extent of its performance; and most importantly (3) to assess which interventions and types of support are most effective (Matthews and Easton 2010).

A further strength of this model is the potential for the women's service to raise awareness with key agencies such as the police. TW Leeds and WATW have both developed strong links with the police, raising awareness about the experiences of women as victims of violence and coercion and how this relates to their involvement in offending behaviour. WATW has also been proactive in developing links with policymakers and politicians, and are communicating with local antisocial behaviour teams about the consequences of punitive approaches to women offenders and women involved in prostitution.

Multi-agency partnerships

While multi-agency working has been used for some time to provide community-based support for groups including those with mental health problems, the introduction of the Crime and Disorder Act in 1998 provided a statutory focus on the role of partnership-working in tackling issues related to crime reduction. Over the last 15 years, there has been a proliferation of multi-agency partnerships dealing with issues such as the identification and management of prolific offenders or perpetrators of antisocial behaviour, as well as the identification and support of victims of violence, vulnerable adults or children at risk of harm.

In general, multi-agency partnership models operate as a hub where referrals can be made to a group of practitioners from across a range of statutory and non-statutory services. Needs assessments for further support can be undertaken, and onward referrals to one or more specialist agencies can be made. Such approaches are generally characterised by higher caseloads and infrequent office-based contacts with clients, and rarely is any direct intervention provided (Wolff et al. 1997).

Multi-agency partnerships can also sometimes utilise case conferences, where individuals are referred to a panel of members, usually from key statutory and non-statutory agencies. At the conference, panel members identify an individual's key needs and work to facilitate rapid access into appropriate support services. When well established, multi-agency partnership groups such as these often have formal information-sharing protocols and service-level agreements with key agencies in order to protect service users, to overcome problems with access criteria and to streamline rapid access into support.

While an element of multi-agency support is often a feature of many exiting models, in some instances exiting support is brokered at a central organisation to be delivered by other services. This type of exiting support usually consists of some form of needs assessment, a service delivery plan, referral to services and monitoring by a care coordinator. An example of this type of approach was Safe Exit in East London, which ceased operation in 2013. Rather than being a multi-agency partnership of professionals, Safe Exit accepted referrals and then made onward referrals to multiple services and agencies across the borough as needs were identified. Safe Exit provided a type of care coordination role, but beyond an initial meeting had limited direct contact with women and did not provide any form of key work. Services such as Beyond The Streets provide a similar onward referral service, using telephone or email self-referrals only, and do not function to monitor individual provision or coordinate women's care.

Safe Exit was predominantly a diversion scheme, set up in 2006 by Toynbee Hall, a charity that works to reduce poverty and disadvantage in the East End of London. The main aim of the scheme was to divert women arrested for loitering or soliciting in Tower Hamlets into support services as a way of preventing the cycle of arrest, fines or ASBOs, and further arrests that women involved in street prostitution experience. Women who came through the scheme were predominantly vulnerable women with problematic drug use. Many had serious health issues, were homeless or without stable housing, and had complex relationships with family and partners.

The Safe Exit Diversion Scheme offered women arrested for prostitution-related offences an alternative to appearing in court. Women who agreed to participate were bailed at the police station to appear at court at a later date, usually in about five weeks. During this time, women were required to attend two appointments – the first to complete an assessment with the Safe Exit Diversion Scheme worker and the second to attend a first appointment at an appropriate service before their court date. Should women complete the diversion, they were not required to attend court and the prosecutor discontinued the case. Between 2006 and 2009, 84 women were referred to the scheme a total of 435 times. The average number of referrals was five, but one woman had been through the scheme 19 times in this three-year period (Rice 2010).

The initial assessment interview focused on the women's priorities. Women were then provided a referral to the support service that would best be able to help them. Given the high number of women presenting with substance misuse and mental health issues, frequent referrals were made to Compass ISIS, a local, specialist, women-only health service. Women were then required to 'meaningfully engage' with the identified support service at a further appointment. The aim of the second appointment was to encourage women to develop key working relationships with services that women were either unaware of or had only had minimal contact with, through outreach, for example.

There was a view among stakeholders who participated in an evaluation of the scheme that some of those who did not engage with the scheme were possibly the most vulnerable. As a result, the scheme worker took a much more active role in encouraging participation through following up individual women (Rice 2010). The evaluation also recommended increasing the number of appointments to three, to further encourage women's engagement with support, particularly among those women referred through the scheme several times.

While a number of women who were involved with the Safe Exit Diversion Scheme made positive changes in their lives, it is unclear to what extent the scheme actually enabled these developments. The evaluation of the scheme recognised that Safe Exit operated within a particular environment and that structural and practical issues interacted with women's motivation and opportunity to change (Rice 2010). The re-referral of women to the Safe Exit Diversion Scheme was indicative of the limits of such a programme. While it offered a much-needed and pragmatic intervention, it was not able to provide the long-term, individually focused support that might meet women's needs to exit. Although the Safe Exit Scheme was considered a positive intervention, stakeholders felt its ability to achieve its key outcomes was heavily reliant on the services to which women were referred, many of which were already at full capacity. Indeed, women in our study indicated that while they were diverted away from prosecution through the Safe Exit scheme, they were unable to make a permanent and sustained exit from prostitution for a number of reasons.

One of the primary reasons why women found permanent exit difficult was problems with housing and accommodation. Over half (51 per cent) of the women who had been referred through the Safe Exit Diversion Scheme were homeless (25 per cent) or living in hostel accommodation (26 per cent). That accommodation problems provide a specific barrier to exit has already been discussed, but within this context these problems were of a very particular nature. Women involved in the study found temporary accommodation in a women-only hostel in the borough. This hostel was located in the heart of the red light district. Women housed here were frequently drug users involved in prostitution. According to women's accounts, abusive and exploitative men frequently waited outside the hostel for women, either to sell them drugs or to engage them in prostitution-related activities. Women who were attempting to exit found this a difficult environment within which to remain motivated. Nonetheless, several of the women interviewed reported that they had done so, and had stayed out of prostitution and away from involvement in substance misuse for many years. These women also reported, however, that they had lived in this temporary accommodation for over four years, and that there had been no support offered to them to assist them to move out of an environment where lapse and relapse were extremely likely. The experiences of these women go some way towards explaining the high levels of re-referral to the scheme, an issue that may be faced by other onward referral/multi-agency-style programmes.

The multi-agency/onward referral model can be considered to have a number of strengths. It is perhaps a pragmatic solution, or can act as a first stage to the development of more integrated, individualised services where there has previously been no coordinated support on offer. Such a model can also develop information-sharing and expertise; assist in the pooling of resources; raise awareness of the needs of women involved in prostitution; act as a signposting and referral agency; identify barriers to women accessing services; and identify gaps in provision or over-subscribed services. Such an approach, particularly when an element of diversion from the criminal justice system is involved, may offer preliminary alternatives to punitive and enforcement-focused approaches to women involved in street prostitution.

In the longer term, however, this type of approach has a number of weaknesses. The high rates of attrition and re-referral may have a number of causes. Perhaps most important is the experience of individual women within this model. When asked about their preferences for service delivery in relation to their attempts to exit prostitution, a number of women indicated a dislike for onward referrals, as they felt they were being passed from service to service. As one woman that we interviewed explained:

> People tend to then think, you know, that they're just passed on to somebody else and passed on to somebody else and like, you go to somebody and 'Oh I'll refer you away', do you know what I mean and it's like, they're passing, people, you know, people could then think 'Oh they're passing the buck', you know what I mean?

Women involved in prostitution may experience a number of challenges when presented with this approach. Engaging with a number of new services may prove difficult for women who may not have sufficient self-confidence or the personal resources to locate services and feel confident to attend them. This might also be exacerbated by the prospect of having to face assessments at each new service, with the likelihood of having to repeat painful experiences. Chaotic women may also find it difficult to keep track of appointments, workers, phone numbers, opening hours and addresses, particularly when needing to engage with a number of different services. The onward referral or multi-agency model may therefore have the effect of setting the most vulnerable women up to fail, as they do not have the sufficient help-seeking skills or capacity to navigate an already complicated system of provision.

The multi-agency model is also limited by the local availability of support and the extent to which the referral agency or partnership can establish constructive relationships with these providers. Even if productive relationships are formed, the lack of capacity of the partnership or hub agency to influence funding decisions or access criteria may mean that referral services are unable to meet the needs of the women involved. Equally, the achievement of key outcomes for each woman is dependent on service delivery beyond the control of the referring organisation.

Another key challenge faced by many multi-agency partnerships is how to negotiate appropriate disclosure between agencies. An evaluation of the prolific offender scheme in London, for example, documented the dilemma that drug services faced when probation requested information about an offender's progress (Easton 2007). Other evaluations of multi-agency partnerships have also identified problems emerging from the competing priorities, varying criteria and conflicting approaches of the different representative organisations. Particular problems existed where statutory enforcement or social care agencies such as the police, probation, social services or health services were required to work in partnership with third sector organisations to provide support for vulnerable groups (Easton and Matthews 2008).

Such partnerships also often suffer problems with communication between partners or may struggle to agree a course of action (Crawford 1998). For women working with multiple agencies, it can be difficult to build trust, while a lack of accountability can prevent the development of an effective therapeutic alliance. Such models also face challenges in dealing with complex cases, such as obtaining housing or mental health support for women who are still using drugs. While the multi-agency model may be able to target multiple needs, the approach is generally not flexible or robust enough to effectively facilitate women exiting prostitution. As a result, despite a partnership's efforts to provide a range of support, a woman may not be able to move beyond her involvement in prostitution, and may be held to blame for her lack of progress, rather than her inability to exit being seen as a result of the limitations of this type of approach.

Case management

Case management approaches have their foundations in the 1970s and 1980s in the US, when psychiatric care was deinstitutionalised and specialist provision for social issues related to ageing, mental health issues and problematic drug use was expanded (Partridge 2004; Rapp 1998; Rothman 1992). Contemporary case management has many applications, and there are significant variations in how case management is both organised and delivered depending upon the needs of the service users and the balance between service user needs and organisational priorities (Partridge 2004). Case management approaches are now widely used both in community care and community corrections, particularly as a way of delivering assistance where people have multiple needs (Ballew and Mink 1996; Rayner 2006; Rothman 1992; Stephens et al. 1991; Vanderplasschen et al. 2004).

As a result of these various approaches, establishing a clear and comprehensive definition of case management is not easy (Partridge 2004). However, a recent review of case management approaches to homelessness in the US, UK, EU and Australia described case management in the following terms:

> The case manager is a friendly professional who can assess and respond to the totality of a person's assistance needs including negotiation of the obstacles interfering with the person's ability to meet their own needs. The case manager uses tools and professional expertise to plan and coordinate a response to these needs within available resources, and to help the person wherever possible develop their capacity for independence. Case management is a professional care service characterised by:
>
> 1. Stability, reliability, continuity, advocacy, and empathy;
> 2. Professional expertise (advanced assessment, communication and relationship skills; knowledge of resource availability and personal or official links with providers);

3. Defined boundaries, honesty and client-directed goal orientation.

(Gronda 2009: 30–31)

In general, the key elements of a case management approach include assessment, planning, coordination, monitoring and evaluation (Agranoff 1977; Evashwick 1997; Moxley 1989; Rose 1992). However, central to such an approach is the role of case managers in accessing and sometimes directly delivering services to clients (Hasenfeld 1983). It is in this regard that case management approaches can vary significantly, depending on the nature and extent of the case manager's involvement. According to Levine and Flemming (1985), for example, there are two broad models of case management: a 'generalist' approach, where one case manager is responsible for all aspects of client care, and a 'specialist' model, where several different practitioners are involved to deliver specific case management functions. Similarly, Hepworth and Larsen (1992) suggest that case management can provide 'simple brokerage of service provision' at one end of the continuum to 'personal involvement' at the other. Ross (1980) argues that there are three types of case management: 'minimal'; 'co-ordination' and 'comprehensive'. The comprehensive model involves the case manager in direct intervention with the client in a similar way to Levine and Flemming's (1985) 'generalist' model. For the purposes of this analysis, it is the 'generalist' approach to case management that is our main point of reference throughout this section.

Adopting a case management approach of this type is considered to have numerous benefits: for example, it offers a single point of accountability, coordination and follow-through, and is able to provide important therapeutic outcomes, including improved independence, self-responsibility and self-care. Case management approaches are also thought to improve overall project management and system improvement, particularly in relation to the allocation of resources, and as such it can also act as a mechanism to contain costs by avoiding duplication and increasing efficiency and effectiveness (Gronda 2009).

One of the most frequently cited reasons for adopting case management is the complex and fragmented nature of the system of support services and the difficulties faced by some individuals in seeking support for themselves in this environment (Ballew and Mink 1996; Case Management Society of Australia 2004; Eustace and Clarke 2005; Rothman 1992; Upston 1994). A key role of case managers is therefore to assist the client to navigate support services, to identify 'gaps' in service delivery and to work towards improving available support (Austin and McClelland 2000). This aspect of case management is described by McDonald and Coventry (2009) as the 'second order' of relationship work within case management, as it requires case managers to build effective partnerships with other service providers.

Recently, case management approaches have begun to be adopted by services supporting women exiting prostitution, and the research underlying this has come into contact with a wide range of services that deliver exiting support using a case management model. These services include the LEA and the Poppy Project at Eaves in South London, CRI Women's Service in Leeds, Trust in South London, Catch 22/3D in Southampton, Streetreach in Doncaster, SWOPP in Sheffield, Make a Change in Ipswich (Poland et al. 2008; Ward 2007), the Chrysalis Project in South London (Easton and Matthews 2012), and the Routes Out Partnership in Glasgow (Matthews and Easton 2010).

In 2006, following the deaths of five women involved in street prostitution, the Ipswich Crime and Disorder Reduction Partnership produced a five-year prostitution strategy which centred around adopting a case management approach to exiting. Central to the strategy was the development of a meaningful pathway out of street prostitution through the provision of individually focused multi-agency case conferences to coordinate the provision of drug treatment, health services, accommodation and other interventions. The experience of Ipswich showed that vulnerable women faced significant barriers to exiting street prostitution even when their lives were at risk. Initially these were identified as problems associated with substance misuse and homelessness, but after further investigation it became apparent that a number of women were involved in coercive and exploitative relationships which maintained them in prostitution.

A similar approach has been adopted in Glasgow since the establishment of the Routes Out Intervention Partnership in 2000, in which a partnership between Strathclyde Police, Glasgow Addiction

Services and Glasgow City Council has taken a proactive, integrated, multi-agency approach to reduce street prostitution in the city. The Routes Out service now provides drop-in and outreach services as well as case management support to help women exit prostitution. While the Routes Out partnership has been operating since 2000, there have been a number of recent changes to the manner in which exiting support is delivered in the city.

The original model was based on a 'Violence Against Women' agenda. This approach differed significantly from other mainstream approaches in Scotland. More recently, however, there has been an attempt to integrate the drop-in service with an exiting service as well as the adoption of a case management approach (Matthews and Easton 2011). Attention has also shifted towards women working indoors, because of a noticeable shift in the location of prostitution in the city and an increasing awareness of the movement of women between off-street and on-street prostitution (Easton and Matthews 2012).

Generally, the case management approach involves direct one-to-one support for women providing onward referral and specialist support, such as counselling, psychotherapy and helping with substance misuse. A feature common to each of the exiting projects is the importance of the relationship between the service user and the key worker. The 'generalist' model emphasises the personal relationship that develops between the case manager and service user over time (Frank and Gunderson 1990). A central element of this approach, according to Mead and Copeland (2000), is the role of the key worker in fostering hope. According to the recovery paradigm, support should 'creatively help a person reconstruct a life narrative that is defined by hope, challenge, accountability, mutual relationship and an evolving self concept' (Mead and Copeland 2000: 320). They suggest: 'The desire to change is nurtured through the relationship, not dictated by one person's plan for another' (ibid.: 321). The advantage of the case management approach is that it provides an individualised programme of support tailored to the needs and aspirations of each individual. It is also flexible in terms of the duration of support:

> The finding of persistence and reliability does not imply that everybody needs a *long* period of case management. Rather it

implies that case management durations must be individually negotiated with reference to the person receiving assistance and a realistic level of self-care as an outcome goal.

(Gronda 2009: 11)

It has been argued that 'arbitrarily imposed case management durations may be inefficient if they end the relationship prematurely' and that 'multi-disciplinary case management teams are most cost-effective for working with people requiring complex service responses' (Gronda 2009: 11). Case management is particularly appropriate in situations in which a person is facing multiple, simultaneous problems, and has not only the task of managing each problem, and the interrelationship of the problems, but also the interrelationship of the assistance providers. While most services providing support for women involved in prostitution have some multi-agency links with benefits and housing agencies, usually regarding practical matters, the case management approach takes this further and strategically develops links with gender-specific support, such as specialist counselling or psychotherapy, which can help women to heal after trauma.

Case management often involves a staged approach rather than simply offering unstructured 'solutions' or assuming that women who do not respond to treatment are 'failures' or 'resistant'. Rather, case management aims to take a reasoned, proactive and responsive approach, utilising understanding of the way in which women exit. A multi-agency approach may randomly offer 'solutions' to women, but a key difference of the case management approach is that it is much more sensitive and has accountability built in. Most importantly, those agencies and key workers that adopt a case management approach tend to believe that people can radically change their lives, and that exiting is both possible and desirable.

While each of the services delivering exiting support relies to a differing degree on the availability and suitability of local statutory and non-statutory service provision, a key advantage of services operating using a case management approach is that they are able to identify and evidence key gaps in provision, and may in some cases have the resources, reputation or budgets available to commission services where needs are unmet (see Gronda 2009).

Conclusion

Although each of these models provides some form of support for women who wish to exit, there is very little doubt that a comprehensive and integrated case management approach is the preferred option, particularly when it is underpinned by a strong belief in the possibility of change. However, each of the approaches, it has been suggested, has certain positive features, and in an ideal situation the aim would be to draw upon these positive strands in each approach. The harm minimisation plus model is important because it provides initial support and provides the basis for developing a relationship of mutual trust between the agency and women involved in prostitution. In as much as harm minimisation services are able to address immediate needs and help women overcome some of the barriers to exiting, they provide a positive and useful service. However, there is a need to build upon these developments and to facilitate exiting rather than seeing such support as a means to perpetuate women in prostitution. The multi-agency approach provides the basis for developing a wide-ranging strategy capable of addressing women's various needs. The woman-centred approach emphasises the need to develop not only gender specific forms of support but also to recognise that women involved in prostitution often require specialist forms of support and treatment; while the case management approach emphasises the need for a proactive, strategic and individually tailored solution.

Bringing these different approaches together in a more integrated, specialised and structured fashion would involve linking harm minimisation more directly with exiting, establishing a range of responsive and effective set of agencies while remaining sensitive to the specificity of prostitution. The work of the Make a Change team in Ipswich and the Routes Out team in Glasgow provides two examples of how exiting work can be effectively delivered in practice, and while both examples acknowledge that there is room for improvement, both also demonstrate initiative, innovation and commitment to exiting.

In Ipswich, there has been significant local commitment to developing a strategic approach aimed at eliminating street prostitution. In 2007 the Joint Agency Strategy Group (JASG) was developed to meet this objective. The JASG involved a partnership between Suffolk

Constabulary, Suffolk Primary Care Trust, Norfolk and Suffolk Probation Trust, Ipswich Borough Council and other local agencies and voluntary sector organisations. In addition to this multi-agency strategic partnership, Ipswich has a dedicated exiting intervention team called Make a Change (MAC). This has a specific remit to provide interventions to support women in leaving prostitution, and to prevent children and young people becoming sexually exploited and involved in prostitution in the future. A development manager oversees two teams of specialist practitioners who deliver direct support work to service users, assisting them in their access of practical support and working with them on issues that relate to emotional well-being. Senior practitioners from the team also have responsibility for awareness-raising and training across the county.

In Ipswich, partnership working around prostitution is well developed, with inter-agency coordinated meeting panels established for both adults and young people. These meetings take referrals for individual women and a multi-agency panel identifies and begins to address their support needs. The MAC also has strong partnership arrangements with two dedicated police officers within the team, a strategic commitment to improving the police response to prostitution through a focus on enforcement activities in relation to demand for prostitution, and by relocating responsibility for prostitution and child sexual exploitation to officers within public protection and victim care (Poland et al. 2012).

Glasgow has long provided a drop-in service for women involved in street prostitution at Base 75 and longer-term exiting support for women who want to leave through the Routes Out Intervention team. However, recent developments in the city have gone some way to developing a more integrated and strategic approach. The Glasgow approach has streamlined provision between outreach, drop-in and case-managed exiting support, with all women using the drop-in service at Base 75 being provided with a one-to-one meeting with an exiting specialist. There is also a much closer relationship between policing and exiting work. As well as established strategic links with the police, there are now two female police officers linked directly into the work of Routes Out. This has improved the flow of information between exiting support and the police, increased support for women in custody or who experience domestic or sexual violence, and increased intelligence-gathering about kerb-crawling.

The service has adopted a 'generalist' case management approach. However, women involved with social work or addictions services often have a 'specialist' case manager already. Information is shared between Routes Out and case managers in other services, with a positive focus on the provision of support rather than on enforcement or punishment. Routes Out is available to provide case management for women who drop out of mainstream services or for women who prefer to receive specialist support. This approach has been facilitated by the adoption of a strategic approach to violence against women in many mainstream services across Glasgow. Specialist provision has also been commissioned across the city to support women who have experienced trauma or who require psychological or counselling support.

A key focus of the work in Glasgow is to prevent women from becoming involved in prostitution in the first place. A growing programme of outreach has been established to ensure that even women not accessing the drop-in service are aware of the potential risks and harms of their involvement and of the availability of support to exit. Outreach workers also link with the police to gather intelligence about kerb-crawlers and potentially vulnerable women. Glasgow also recognises the importance of adopting a preventative approach with vulnerable young women by providing advice and support through the Young Women's Project (YWP). The YWP is run by Glasgow Social Work Services and provides intensive support for approximately 30 vulnerable young women aged 12–18 years, and has adopted a case management approach that provides a combination of individual, group work, workshops and family work coordinated by a key worker. The service also works in partnership with key agencies across Glasgow to link young women with mainstream provision, and with the Barnardo's Street Team who provide an outreach and drop-in service to vulnerable young people at risk of sexual exploitation.

The strengths of both of these approaches are that they have adopted a strategic case management approach that incorporates an inter-agency focus on exiting. As a result, both have developed integrated support from drop-in and outreach through to the development of meaningful routes out of prostitution. They prioritise the prevention of new entrants from taking up prostitution and have developed provision for children and young people at risk of sexual exploitation. Both have also begun to address the demand for prostitution through initiatives to tackle kerb-crawling and through community engagement and awareness-raising efforts. They are also beginning to consider and address the relationship between on- and off-street prostitution and the needs of women involved in less visible forms of prostitution, particularly those involving contacts made via the internet. While significantly different, the two approaches provide examples of how local exiting provision might be configured to best support women in their desire to cease their involvement in prostitution.

6
Exiting, Policy and Practice

Introduction

It is remarkable how long it has taken for us to take exiting from prostitution seriously. However, we have moved tentatively over the past decades from seeing women involved in prostitution as offenders, then as victims, and more recently as a group of people with agency who are willing and able to take control of their lives and leave prostitution.

For many people in the UK the murders of five women in Ipswich, and the subsequent efforts to help women involved in prostitution in the area to exit and thereby to remove prostitution from the streets, changed their attitudes towards both prostitution and exiting. These sentiments were reflected in the influential Corston Report (2007), which called for a radical rethink of the treatment of women involved in prostitution.

> The tragic series of murders in Suffolk during December 2006 rightly focussed public attention on these women as women first and foremost – someone's daughter, mother, girlfriend, then as victims – exploited by men damaged by abuse and drug addiction. These are among the women that society must support and help to establish themselves in the community.
>
> (Corston 2007: i)

Support for exiting has come nationally from official bodies, which have come to recognise that the best ways of reducing the harms associated with prostitution is to help women to leave prostitution.

Thus, the government consultation paper *Paying the Price* (Home Office 2004) identified helping women to exit prostitution as a priority, while the subsequent *Coordinated Prostitution Strategy* (Home Office 2006) identified drug addiction and homelessness as key barriers to exiting prostitution. Although both of these reports provide an important endorsement of exiting, the strategies they propose are largely administrative and pragmatic and pay little attention to the emotional and relational elements of desistance.

These official reports draw heavily on the widely referenced study by Hester and Westmarland (2004), who note in their evaluation of five exiting projects that:

> With regards to exiting, the profiles of the women using these five projects showed that most of the women were trying to exit prostitution or had tried in the past on one or more occasion (69%, 128/186). Less than a third had never tried to exit (31%, 58/186). If women did not want to nor felt ready to exit prostitution, the support interventions worked as a form of harm minimisation. The fact that the majority of the women had attempted to exit also highlights the need for projects to support women towards exiting prostitution, rather than focusing solely on harm minimisation.
>
> (Hester and Westmarland 2004: 85)

However, they also claim, like many others, that: 'moving towards exiting and actually exiting from prostitution is a long and complex process'. Our research, however, suggests that this is not the case, for many are able to leave prostitution once they have appropriate support and suitable conditions, combined with the commitment to exit. Moreover, as we have seen, some women are 'self-exiters', requiring minimal levels of formal support.

In a similar review prepared for the Ministry of Justice in New Zealand, Mayhew and Mossman (2007) note that many women involved in prostitution, in principle at least, want to exit. As they note: 'routes out for different women will be conditioned by their type of involvement in the sex industry'. Like many other commentators, they adopt a staged model of change. We have suggested that this model, which is widely featured in the literature, does not square very well with the accounts provided by the women in our sample who have exited. In reality, many of these women appear to be at a number of stages simultaneously, while others skip 'stages' or have repeated lapses. Therefore, as a basis of analysis and intervention we do not favour a stages approach, particularly in its more rigid forms such as that developed by Prochaska et al. (1992).

Researchers in other countries such as Sweden have also examined the process of exiting and provided resources for exiting programmes. Mansson and Hedin (1999), in their study of women leaving prostitution, aim to present an integrated model that combines structure and agency. In relation to structural prerequisites they identify work, housing and education. However, they point out that the discursive and normative context within which decisions are made is important. Mansson and Hedin also stress the role of close relationships and social networks in facilitating change, particularly in relation to parents, partners and children (Hedin and Mansson 2003). At the same time, they argue that the individuals' drive and abilities are also important, as are their degrees of resistance, initiative and creativity. Thus they suggest that:

> Among these internal driving forces is the ability to dream and fantasize. It is often the case that people who have experienced much frustration and disappointment do not dare to dream or plan because of the risk of another failure. They take one day at a time, not daring to hope for the future. However, the ability to hold on to one's dreams can turn out to be crucial to change and growth. As we know it, the woman's ability to escape an unbearable reality through fantasy plays a major role during their time in prostitution. Moreover, their ability to dream and fantasize is also important after the breakaway.
>
> (Mansson and Hedin 1999: 74)

We have noted above the importance of hope in allowing women to visualise alternatives, and have suggested that hope signifies the realisation that an alternative future is not only desirable but also achievable.

There is also a growing interest in exiting in America. Although selling sex remains criminalised in most states, and women involved in prostitution are seen primarily as offenders, several research studies and organisations are beginning to address the issue of exiting. One ethnographic study of a residential programme for women exiting prostitution in a large American city found that the organisational structure in which women are 'treated' plays an important role in their ability and willingness to change (Oselin 2009).

Canadian researchers have examined the role of housing and criminalisation as barriers to exiting prostitution (PAAFE 2005). Based on a survey of 30 women, they found that the majority (25) had tried to leave prostitution at least once. The reasons given for returning to the street included problems of drug addiction, the need for money, feeling lonely and coercion from partners. Nineteen women indicated that they had been refused employment because of their criminal history, while many experienced some form of homelessness prior to and during their involvement in prostitution. The researchers provide a number of recommendations for addressing these barriers to exiting, including creating 'first step' housing for women with addictions and to expunge criminal records within two years of application.

There is also evidence that the issue of exiting prostitution has become an item on the agenda of different local authorities in the UK and amongst various support agencies. Two of the most notable examples of local authority action and intervention are Ipswich and Glasgow. The initiative in Ipswich involved a combination of inter-agency cooperation and a case management approach and has proved successful in substantially reducing street prostitution. Subsequently attention has turned to women who are involved in off-street prostitution (Poland et al. 2008; Ward 2007).

Glasgow developed a pioneering exiting programme in the 1990s. Its Routes Out project received widespread acclaim for its efforts to help women leave prostitution (Swift 2005). However, the early developments of this approach were based on Judith Herman's 'Trauma and Recovery' model, and consequently there was an emphasis on long-term counselling and treatment. In recent years, however, Glasgow has modified its exiting strategy, which now operates with a more integrated proactive approach to exiting that is designed to help women leave prostitution in the shortest possible time (Matthews and Easton 2010).

As we have seen, there are various support agencies that now include exiting as part of their service. These agencies tend to operate with different models of change, and exiting itself is given a different emphasis by these agencies. It is significant, however, that the UK Network of Sex Work Projects, which represents in excess of 100 support agencies in the UK, has produced a good practice guide to exiting (UKNSWP 2008). The guidance centres around provision of a comprehensive and user-friendly drug service, addressing the issue of criminal convictions, promoting education, training and employment, as well as providing different forms of accommodation depending on the need and situation of different women. Health issues are also identified as a major barrier to exiting, as are accessing benefits and receiving financial advice. Also noted are the importance of family issues, stigma, and training for exiting staff, so they are sensitive to providing the right kind of support to women who want to exit.

Thus it can be seen both nationally and internationally that exiting is moving up the social and political agenda, and that different agencies and organisations are beginning to grapple with the complex issues of how people change. There are some areas of agreement amongst these different bodies of what needs to be done to facilitate exiting, but there is considerable uncertainty about which exiting strategies are most effective and how they should be implemented and assessed.

However, it is becoming increasingly clear that there are two compelling rationales for developing and supporting exiting strategies: one is associated with humanism and issues of choice and self-determination, the other is centred on the cost-effectiveness of intervention. The implication of these two rationales is, first, that exiting provides potentially enormous personal and social benefits for many of the women involved in prostitution; second, that it offers the prospect of substantial savings to the taxpayer, and is likely to be of interest to those motivated by fiscal concerns. However, in combination, exiting provides a positive option that is capable of providing a number of wide-ranging benefits.

Choices, rights and self-determination

It has often been pointed out that women or girls entering prostitution are either subject to 'drift', persuasion or coercion (Matthews 2008). Because many enter as children, it is difficult to maintain the notion that this is as a result of 'free' or 'rational' choice. Others, as we know, enter prostitution because of addiction or because they are homeless or runaways. Thus, rather than seeing entry into prostitution as a result of 'choice', it often seems to be the case that women become involved in prostitution when they run out of choices. As Sheila Jeffreys has argued:

> The language of choice puts the responsibility of prostitution upon women. Men's abuse of women involved in prostitution is explained in terms of the actions of the women they abuse, i.e. a woman's choice to be there. In relation to other areas of violence against women, asking the question of why women stay – or in other ways putting the responsibility on the victim – is recognised by feminists as victim blaming. Only in relation to prostitution is this still seen as a legitimate tactic.
>
> (Jeffreys 1997: 139)

In many ways the concepts of 'choice' and indeed consent are inappropriate when applied to women's exiting or involvement in prostitution (Hunter and Cowan 2007). However, the first time that women involved in prostitution begin to exercise real choice is when they decide to confront the barriers that face them and make a decision to leave. Women in our study talked of taking 'control' in a search for real alternatives. For example, one woman who was in the process of exiting and who received some comments from the interviewer about her remarkably positive outlook replied:

> You got to, because you know what, if you don't get rid of all that anger and that hate, it will crack you up. And I ain't letting them win. I'm winning [laughs]. 'Cos I feel that if I don't do that then they still got control and the only person that is gonna control my life is me.

It is, however, ironic that some individuals and groups that claim they see 'choice' as a major consideration seem to want women to make the choice to remain in prostitution. Given that there are strong indicators that many women involved in prostitution would like to leave given the opportunity, it might be expected that those organisations that claim to defend the rights of women involved in prostitution would act to support women in this endeavour. Unfortunately, the leading national and international prostitute rights organisations seem to be preoccupied with normalising prostitution and promoting the sex industry.

Many of the women who want to leave prostitution, as we have seen in this and other studies, want to change a situation that they have come to see as damaging and exploitative for a more positive and rewarding way of life (Irving and Laing 2013). For many of these women, this may be the first time that they have exercised a significant degree of choice in their lives and have been able to exercise some self-determination.

The economics of exiting

Apart from the human costs of prostitution there are also financial implications. Clearly the cost of treatment, support services and the like over time can be considerable.

However, estimating the economic cost of prostitution is very difficult, but a basic calculation indicates that the potential savings associated with women exiting are significant. One of the few studies that has attempted to estimate the cost–benefit of exiting is that conducted in Ipswich in an evaluation of the inter-agency case management approach, which was designed to promote exiting in 2007. This study indicated that the intervention achieved considerable long-term benefits, with an approximate saving of £2 for every £1 spent within the strategy (Poland et al. 2012). A major part of this was a result of reducing the number of arrests, prosecutions and time spent in prison. Overall it is estimated that there was a 55 per cent reduction in criminal justice costs following the introduction of the 'routes out' strategy. Further cost savings are also anticipated as a result of the preventative work now being undertaken. There are other gains in relation to increased community support (Ward 2007).

The most significant savings in Ipswich were a function of a decrease in the number of cases prosecuted between 2006 and 2011, which decreased from 255 to 149. These offences included not only soliciting but also theft, criminal damage and assault, although the number of Class A drug possession cases increased slightly. In addition, there was an increase in the number of women housed, while a recent Department of Health report (2012) claimed that dealing with violence against women in prostitution cost the criminal justice system, health agencies and social services £2.1 billion a year.

Calculating the cost of drug treatment in relation to exiting is difficult. Much will depend on the type of addiction, the length and type of treatment provided and the cost of alternative medications, such as methadone. Some forms of addiction are more readily catered for than others, while few agencies deal effectively with forms of poly-drug use.

The various forms of drug treatment available are the use of opiate substitutes, such as methadone, detox and residential rehabilitation. The cost of placing someone on methadone was estimated to be approximately £3,000 per person per year by the National Treatment Outcome Study (Gossop et al. 2001). There are in excess of 170,000 people in the UK given regular doses of methadone, and there was a 60 per cent increase in methadone prescriptions between 2003 and 2007 (Byford et al. 2013).

Although widely used, some doubts have been expressed about the appropriateness and effectiveness of methadone. Critics have pointed out that between 5 and 10 per cent of people addicted to heroin fail to respond to methadone, while other forms of treatment such as injectable heroin are held to be more cost-effective (Doran 2008). Various respondents in our study reported that they continued to use heroin alongside methadone. Others reported various side-effects, such as drowsiness, stomach cramps, constipation, increased apathy and decreased sex drive.

As an alternative, a 12-week detox programme costs between £6,000 and £12,000, depending on the complexity of the person's needs. Many people, however, do not complete the programme, and it is reported to have a relatively low success rate (Warren et al. 2006). In contrast, the most effective form of treatment is held to be residential rehabilitation, but very few women in our sample were offered this form of treatment. This is probably because the cost is between £600 to £700 per person per week. In general, only better-off women tend to receive residential rehabilitation.

Thus it would appear that the overriding rationale for prescribing methadone is that it is significantly cheaper than other forms of treatment that are designed to achieve abstinence. Rather than providing long-term treatment, it involves the replacement of one form of addiction with another. Therefore, there are issues about the nature of drug treatment not only of opiate users but also those who are addicted to cocaine and cannabis, as well as the many poly-drug users. Thus, 'problematic' drug use amongst women involved in prostitution is unlikely to be solved simply by implementing 'fast-track' services, as some maintain. Research on the drug services available to women involved in street prostitution suggests that there remain a number of organisational barriers to accessing drug services in the UK. These include a lack of flexibility, restrictive opening times, problems arising from missed appointments, lack of childcare provision, a lack of support to address related issues such as homelessness, and a lack of ongoing support and aftercare (DrugScope 2012).

While the cost savings and effectiveness of different forms of drug treatment is in need of review, there can be little doubt that there is a potential saving in relation to exiting in cases where children are removed from care and reunited with their mothers. As we have seen, the process of re-establishing relationships with children is in some cases an important feature of the exiting process. The Department of Children Schools and Families estimates that it costs £25,000–£30,000 per year to place a child in foster care (Holmes et al. 2009). The costs will vary in relation to the type of care provided.

The health care costs associated with prostitution are considerable. As we have seen, women involved in prostitution experience a range of recurring health care issues mainly in the form of sexually transmitted infections, injecting site abscesses, gynaecological problems and hepatitis B and C. Clearly, reducing the number of sexual contacts is likely to improve health, particularly in cases where condoms are not used, and this will in turn reduce the demand for medical services.

One area where costs might increase at least in the short term is housing. Many women involved in prostitution, as we have noted, are 'homeless'. The provision of different forms of accommodation, whether a hostel, temporary accommodation or longer-term supported independent accommodation, has associated costs. The model utilised in Lambeth, South London, shows how such costs can be minimised through the adoption of a sustainable funding model, involving partnership between the third sector and local authorities (Easton and Matthews 2012). In cases where women are able to take on and maintain a tenancy on their own, costs can be short-term.

Overall, there can be little doubt that significant cost savings can be achieved by developing effective exiting programmes. In many respects, it would appear that exiting provides an option that not only helps the women themselves but also the taxpayer. A more detailed and nuanced mode of calculation is necessary to determine more precisely the exact savings involved, but these rough estimates suggest that such savings may be considerable in the long term.

Rethinking desistance and exiting

In the course of the research, we aimed to examine the various accounts of desistance and exiting that have been presented to date. We were from the outset fairly sceptical of the assumption that there was an explanation of change that would apply equally to all groups in all circumstances, and as the research developed these suspicions were confirmed. We found that neither did the majority of women trying to leave prostitution go through a series of identifiable stages nor did they change in the ways predicted by the major theories. Moreover, the 'stages of change' approaches proved to be unable to provide convincing explanations of how people move from one stage to the next (Sutton 1996).

The three main approaches that we considered included those that focus on 'turning points' presented by Sampson and Laub (1993), the claim that people have to work through their trauma and engage in long-term counselling and therapy in order to move on outlined by Herman (1992; 2003), and the suggestion that in order for people to make positive changes in their lives they need to construct 'redemption scripts' that can connect the past to the present by developing a coherent sense of self (Maruna 2001). In terms of 'turning points', we found that employment paid a minor role in the exiting process for women involved in prostitution, although becoming pregnant and finding a new stable partner can be significant. However, it has been suggested that these structural constraints do not just appear and are not random. Rather, they are often actively sought out by the agents involved. In terms of trauma and the need for counselling and therapy, there were a number of women who had histories of abuse and victimisation who suffered from depression and anxiety, had low self-esteem and could see no way out of their present predicament. It was remarkable, however, that despite the troubled histories and regular exposure to violence and abuse, many women exhibited an impressive degree of resilience and an ability to remain positive and forward-looking. It was also the case that women with psychological problems were in some cases able to exit prostitution without therapy but engaged in some forms of treatment after leaving prostitution. We have noted above, however, that explanations of exiting tend to focus on the most damaged, desperate and disorganised women involved in prostitution, particularly those involved in street prostitution. However, if we are to develop more effective approaches to exiting we need to consider the full range of women involved in prostitution who want to leave, and tailor our explanations and interventions accordingly.

In terms of 'redemption scripts', such a process may be applicable to people moving out of crime, but there was no reference to this type of strategy amongst the women that we interviewed. Instead, we found that the majority of women involved in prostitution who are trying to exit are able to effectively 'knife off' or block out their past, and it is the availability of, and the quality of, both formal and informal support combined with the motivation to change that provides the basic conditions for a successful exiting strategy. We have suggested that there are three main reasons why women exiting prostitution are able to 'misremember' the past. First, the 'self' which engages in prostitution is often a constructed self designed to act out a role in order to manage different buyers in the most effective way. This is, as many women report, an act or a 'performance;' in which they have little or no emotional involvement. In many cases they can effectively disassociate and present a credible persona for the duration of the encounter. In this way they are able to protect and maintain an essential sense of self that exists before, during and after the sex act. Second, the repeated exposure to violence and abuse combined with the physically damaging nature of the activity means that that there are very few 'happy hookers', and that the combination of these pressures makes many women think about exiting on a regular basis. For some, the only way that they can sustain these negative experiences is through the regular use of drugs and alcohol. This also serves as a distancing and coping mechanism. Third, there is often an element of neutralisation. That is, most women realise that they did not 'choose' to become involved in prostitution but that they were coerced, led or encouraged to become involved by past events or the actions of third parties – often at an early age. Therefore, in a sense they are able, with some justification, to reduce their responsibility and realise that they did not so much choose this way of life but rather that it was chosen for them. Once in a position to exercise 'real' choice, they are able to decide in many cases to pursue a life that is more fulfilling and less damaging.

In the literature on exiting and desistance, considerable emphasis is placed on the need to provide 'holistic' support and address women's complex needs. While this is a desirable objective, our research suggests that not all of the women's needs have to be addressed before they are able to leave prostitution; what is required is individual, tailored and coordinated interventions. There is a tendency by some agencies to operate with a 'deficit model', which concentrates on addressing women's problems and difficulties. While this is important, the research suggests that this needs to be accompanied by interventions that aim to build up hope and trust, and encourage the women concerned to develop a positive future-orientated perspective, which involves recognition of their strengths and opportunities. Thus it has been suggested that we replace the deficit model by the Good Lives Model (Ward and Maruna 2007). If the aim is to develop a 'holistic' approach, it is important not only to dwell on the deficiencies, barriers and obstacles to exiting but also to identify individuals' capacities and opportunities. Rather than focusing exclusively on dealing with the various 'needs' that a service user presents, it might be more productive to engage simultaneously in developing a collaborative strategy that is based on the identification of exactly what it would take for her to leave prostitution and what changes she would like to make to her life.

Women and desistance

Our examination of exiting has raised questions about the nature of female desistance. In contrast to Giordano et al. (2002), who suggest that the process of distance is largely similar for both men and women, our study suggests that there are some important differences. These differences, however, may be a function of the focus on desistance from crime and delinquency. Thus there are two questions that need to be addressed. The first is whether the dynamics of moving out of crime and prostitution are essentially the same. Second, whether there are gendered differences involved in making significant changes in lifestyle, attitudes and behaviour.

It would seem that one of the clear findings of our study is that a 'one size fits all' approach to desistance such as that adopted by Prochaska et al. (1992) is inadequate, and that it is important to recognise the specificity of different actors and contexts. Thus desisting from crime is likely to involve different dynamics than those involved in exiting prostitution. Second, the 'routes out' adopted by women involved in prostitution appear different from those adopted by men involved in crime and other deviant activities.

There seem to be four main differences between desistance for men and women. First, informal relations and supports tend to play a more important role for women than men (Hedin and Mansson 2003). Second, when women exit they often seek conventional roles of partner or parent. Third, and relatedly, women are more concerned than male offenders in seeking roles with social approval (McNeill and Weaver 2010). Fourth, there is some evidence that when women decide to change their lifestyle they are able to do so more quickly than their male counterparts. It also appears that engaging in crime and deviant behaviour is a qualitatively different experience for women and men (Corston 2007).

However, it is evident from this study that engaging in prostitution involves a different form of transgression than engaging in conventional forms of crime. The study by McIvor et al. (2004) also draws attention to the gendered social context within which young women offend, identifying the contradictory ways in which gender can influence women's understanding of their offending behaviour. They found that in contrast to young men, young women did not want to identify themselves as persisters even if they had continued offending, suggesting offending has different significance in relation to young men and young women's self identity. As they concluded:

> Assigning the offending to the past rather than acknowledging it as a current or future reality may enable young women to better cope with the tensions that may arise when, on the one hand, society encourages gender equality and, on the other, continues to doubly condemn young women who step beyond their traditional gender roles.
>
> (McIvor et al. 2004)

While engaging in crime is for some young men a way of 'doing masculinity' (Messerschmidt 1993), the same is less frequently the

case for young women. Instead, young women's gender socialisation means that they (and society) view themselves as being 'doubly
deviant', having simultaneously transgressed both social and gender
norms through their involvement in offending (Heidensohn 2006).
Therefore, in relation to women's desistance, the process of reconstructing both the non-offending and the gender role is potentially
more complicated than the same process for men.

Maruna's (2001) classic study of 'making good', for example, suggests that persistent offenders tend to view themselves as determined
by unpleasant pasts or as victims of circumstance, while desisters are
less likely to self-blame and are able to integrate their past, present
and future selves within their narratives. According to Maruna, successful desistance is characterised by 'willful cognitive distortion'
in order that ex-offenders can 'make good' their past bleak experiences and incorporate them into their new life narratives. This was
not necessarily the case for women involved in prostitution. As we
have suggested, many women involved in prostitution are very adept
at emotional management and are able to compartmentalise their
involvement, and in some cases dissociate parts of themselves, in
order to engage in prostitution. In fact, a critical distinction between
those who are able to exit relatively easily and those who find leaving prostitution very difficult may well be a function of their ability
to dissociate and block off the past on one hand while not fully
adopting a prostitute identity on the other.

Our study suggests, therefore, that rather than integrating their
offending pasts women are much more likely to split them off and
manage separate identities. Therefore, while men (and some women
perhaps) can reconstruct their offending behaviour as part of themselves, possibly through their agency (McIvor et al. 2004), women for
whom crime is not a gender-normal behaviour struggle to integrate
this part of themselves. Therefore while men can claim crime as an
aspect of their masculinity, women split off a part of themselves and
perhaps do not accept their deviant behaviour as part of who they are
(McIvor et al. 2004). Women who have had difficult past experiences
of sexual trauma might be very capable of dissociation, protecting
their 'core self' from the damaged identity of sexual abuse, prostitution or crime. Alternatively, other women, who feel they are more
active in their choice to become involved in prostitution and who are
lucky not to experience significant trauma whilst selling sex, might
be able to behave more like Maruna's (2001) ex-offenders, who can

adapt their life stories to accommodate their deviance. While many women are able to exit without significant psychotherapeutic support, perhaps reconciling these fragmented parts of themselves later, there are some women who will experience significant challenges to exit as a result of their dissociation.

Another central theme of Maruna's (2001) work is how offenders manage shame. Shame, he suggests, is caused by 'degradation ceremonies' encountered by men *within* the criminal justice system. Women involved in prostitution are likely to experience high levels of shame. However, the causes of this shame are significantly different. First, women involved in prostitution often have experiences of sexual and domestic violence which are known often to induce a sense of shame in victims. Second, as McIvor et al. (2004) suggest, women are also likely to experience differential levels of shame through their transgression of traditional gender roles. While offending is increasingly recognised as a way of 'doing gender' for men, the same is not true for most women offenders. Indeed, many women's involvement in offending is not performative but rather is a result of their gendered position within the social world, often as victims. For women involved in prostitution, shame is therefore not only about the 'acts' that they commit but also becomes about who they are as a person, thus making the process of identity transformation even more complicated. Women's criminalisation, while perhaps less common, also further compounds these complex experiences of shame.

As we have seen, a significant number of women involved in prostitution aim to adopt traditional gender roles of wife or mother when leaving prostitution. Rumgay (2004) has suggested that common identities such as 'mother' provide women with a skeleton script through which they can claim an alternative, socially approved identity. However, not all women aspire to or are able to achieve such roles. This raises the issue of whether women ascribe to these roles because of the lack of viable alternatives on offer: as we have seen in relation to exiting, for example, the limited emphasis that is placed on finding alternative forms of employment.

Even among those women who drew on traditional scripts of wife or mother, there is a risk of becoming involved in 'unrewarding conventional arrangements' (Rumgay 2004). There were also women in our study who had children permanently removed from their care and were not interested in forming conventional heterosexual relationships after leaving prostitution. For other women their aspirations centred around finding stable accommodation.

As Rumgay (2004) argues, unfamiliarity with the behavioural routines that support such scripts means women can face a challenge to their accomplishment. Women who have not been exposed to traditional scripts, for example, might aspire to them but not have sufficient knowledge of the required behaviour and practices to fulfil them: examples are women who have experienced abusive family relationships or whose parents were themselves involved in prostitution, crime or substance misuse. It is therefore questionable whether women involved in prostitution have access to suitable pro-social 'skeleton scripts'. While these may be available for some women, others might have a limited range of 'scripts' to choose from and poor models of those scripts to draw from. As Giordano et al. (2002) suggest, without a good understanding of what a script involves, women are not able to effectively utilise their new role as a cognitive filter for their decision-making, nor are they convincing to those around them, potentially undermining their efforts to adopt a new role.

Examination of the narratives of women exiting prostitution suggests that there are few alternative scripts for 'replacement selves' for women to choose from. This can be for a number of reasons. Conventional roles might not be accessible or attractive to women exiting prostitution. Women might not be able to form intimate, secure relationships with kind and understanding partners, they might lack trust in men through their experiences in prostitution, they may have children in care with whom they are unable to reconnect, or they might simply not want to have children. Conventional gender roles are also limiting. Needing to care for children, for example, potentially contributes to women being unable to access alternative roles via education or employment. There were, however, women who moved on to exit prostitution without adopting one of these socially determined gender roles. These were women who could be described as going 'off script'.

A central element of any strategy designed to support women's desistance must therefore pay attention to finding meaningful employment and raising women's expectations. Exiting work with women might therefore involve a widening of women's aspirations not just in relation to their employment but also in relation to leisure, where women might connect to new interests and passions and find inspiration to go beyond their gender role and follow lesser-known 'scripts'.

Furthermore, we need to consider how women may be best supported in their attempts to exit. Should interventions aim to correct some of the social inequalities that women experience, or should they assist women to better act out the 'scripts' which society has given them? If desistance theory suggests that desistance is linked to one's access to 'legitimacy packages', such as work, education, marriage and other intimate relationships, how then does desistance work for women whose different social position means they have different access and a different relationship to these resources. And how do women access alternative 'scripts' for 'replacement selves' when opportunities are limited or linked to gender roles that have in the past been unsuitable. Clearly, attempts made by women to desist from offending or exit prostitution are heavily influenced by issues such as gender inequality and gender socialisation. Therefore, just as criminology has begun to examine the context of women's wider experiences of oppression, research on desistance must begin to engage with the gendered experiences that influence women's capacity to desist (Heidensohn 2006).

Developing a model of effective practice

In our review of the different modes of intervention and support, we concluded that each of these models had positive attributes and that the challenge was to develop an approach that could combine elements of these approaches in a way that would promote exiting. As was suggested, the harm minimisation plus model is useful in that it offers critical open access and support for women involved in prostitution and provides essential health care, while referring service users to other support agencies that provide accommodation, drug treatment and the like. The main advantage of such an approach is that it seeks to maintain the health and well-being of women while helping to re-establish trust. It tends to be limited, however, in as much as it is largely reactive and only responds to demands from the women themselves.

The multi-agency model, on the other hand, aims to bring together a range of services in a coordinated way but is not specifically focused on exiting. While services provide cost-effective women-specific support, the absence of a focus on prostitution and the particular needs of women involved in this activity means there is the potential to exclude the most chaotic, vulnerable and marginalised women who experience the greatest harm.

The multi-agency model acts as a referral hub, where the practical needs of women involved in prostitution can be identified and links made with services that can meet these needs. This model, while popular with commissioners, faces a number of challenges, including those commonly experienced by other partnerships: they include, amongst other things, fragmented funding, patchy provision, conflicting access criteria, and problems with communication and disclosure. While it could be argued that such an approach is lower in cost it tends to involve a relatively high drop-out rate. Moreover, this approach is limited in its capacity to reach the most chaotic and marginalised women, particularly those who do not have the self-confidence or personal resources to make and manage contacts with a number of providers at once.

The case management model, on the other hand, has a specific focus on the needs of women involved in prostitution. The case management model provides women with a single point of contact where both the emotional and practical issues related to exiting can be addressed in an individualised, targeted and coordinated manner. Central to this is the keyworker relationship, is the development of a sense of trust. The keyworker also helps the service user navigate support services and identify and overcome gaps in provision. The case management model means greater accountability – both between the exiting service and partner services and between the exiting worker and the service user. Case management has been shown to be cost effective and particularly appropriate in situations in which a person is facing multiple problems. The aim is not only to manage each problem but also the underlying causes of these problems (Gronda 2009).

In drawing the positive elements of these approaches together, we would advocate an integrated model that combines what we have identified as the positive features of the four models that have been identified. Diagrammatically, the approach we would advocate would take the following form (Figure 6.1).

The critical difference between this model and a harm minimisation plus approach is that it is proactive, and that the exiting team works alongside and in conjunction with the support workers.

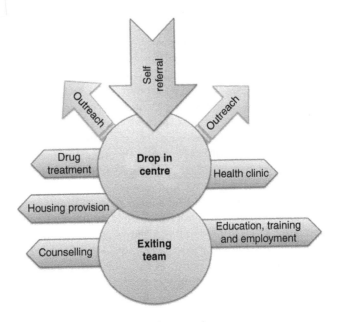

Figure 6.1 A model of an integrated approach

It is important to develop a proactive approach since, as the general literature on desistance points out, the process of change is often characterised by ambivalence and vacillation, and therefore the ability to foster and sustain motivation is central if a significant change is to be realised (Burnett and Maruna 2004). Also, as McNeill (2009) points out, people need to be given realistic alternatives and be allowed to 'discover' that change is possible and achievable. Thus:

> Desistance is also an active process and one in which agency (that is the ability to exercise choice and manage one's own life) is 'discovered'. This necessitates approaches to supervision that are active and participative and that seek to maximise involvement and collaboration. The desistance literature also highlights the need to establish relationships within which attempts to positively influence the offender carry *moral legitimacy* (from the offender's perspective). This again underlines the need for the worker's authority to be exercised in a manner that is clear, explicit and fair. It also points to the importance of offering practical help

to offenders since there is a vital expression of concern for them *as people*, as well as a demonstration of an awareness of their social reality.

(McNeill 2009)

Thus, an effective exiting approach must necessarily move beyond providing a purely pragmatic and instrumental response or only referring people to different agencies. Rather, it is necessary to recognise and convey the rewards for leaving prostitution, and be able to show that other women have overcome similar obstacles to exiting and moved on (McNeill and Weaver 2010).

Desistance-focused practice

In the previous chapters we have been critical of some of the dominant approaches to desistance and exiting and have begun to flesh out an alternative mode of analysis. Moving away from these widely adopted approaches means that we need to take a fresh look at developing policy and practice. In doing so, there is a need to formulate some guiding principles that might allow us to develop more effective forms of practice.

1. Recognise the role of both formal and informal supports and wherever possible maximise the effects of both.
2. Move beyond a 'deficit model' and develop a 'Good Lives Model' focusing on strengths and opportunities.
3. Rather than rely predominantly on instrumental or pragmatic responses recognise the role of developing a positive perspective involving the establishment of hope and rebuilding trust.
4. Recognise that relapses and reversals are a normal feature of the exiting process but work towards ways of managing these setbacks, rather than seeing them as a failure.
5. Develop more proactive exiting strategies rather than purely reactive responses.
6. Do not work on the assumption that exiting is going to be a long-drawn-out process. In many cases it is not.
7. Evaluate exiting interventions not only in terms of those who cease their involvement in prostitution for three months or more but also incorporate 'soft' measures of change, such as decreased

involvement in prostitution and achievements towards rebuilding personal relationships and social lives.
8. Recognise the significance of social contexts and constraints, rather than trying only to 'fix' people.

Needless to say, it is important to build up positive relationships with service users. As has been suggested, the exiting strategy should be worked out collaboratively and goals and objectives as well as the route out need to be specified (McNeill and Weaver 2010). Interventions will need to be individually tailored and take account of each person's capacities and skills, as well as the barriers to change that confront them. Some level of monitoring and evaluation is necessary to determine not only 'what works' but also how and why it works.

The adoption of a proactive case management approach, it has been suggested, provides a form of engagement and supervision which allows the practitioner to act as a 'navigator' rather than an instructor. There is a need to provide continuity and consistency of contact and to build up trust. This is what many of the harm minimisation agencies aim to do. However, the aim is not to try and maintain women in prostitution but rather to encourage them to exit, by assuring them that leaving prostitution is achievable.

In this process there is a need, wherever possible, to reconnect women with family and friends as well as the wider community. These 'significant others' can play a major role in supporting and maintaining an exiting strategy. Developing these forms of social capital should also ideally be linked to employment. Not enough is currently being done in this respect, and our research suggests that women only engage in employment towards the end of the exiting process or after they have left prostitution.

It is indicative that very few women in our sample required counselling or therapy in order to leave prostitution, although some sought counselling after stopping or exiting. This, in turn, involves considerations of whether the person who engages in selling sex identifies herself as a 'prostitute' or 'sex worker'. We need to have an appreciation of the level of immersion in the sex trade that different people have, since we know that this will have a major bearing on their ability to exit. The degree of identification will also be conditioned by their location in the sex industry and by, for example, whether they are involved in on-street or off-street prostitution.

As we have suggested, there are significant differences between routes out for those involved in street and indoor prostitution as well as those who have been trafficked. Women involved in indoor prostitution tend to have more skills, better work histories and greater social capital.

Some unanswered questions

In the course of this examination of women leaving prostitution, our aim has been to shed some light on the processes and practices of exiting. Our study, however, is far from comprehensive or definitive, and more detailed work needs to be carried out in the future. In the course of our investigations a number of challenging and unresolved issues have arisen which require further consideration.

The first concerns the monitoring and evaluation of exiting programmes. Previous research has pointed out that owing to either a lack of funds or a lack of expertise few exiting projects have been rigorously evaluated to date (Hester and Westmarland 2004). Evaluations of exiting projects often operate with relatively crude criteria of whether the women involved in the project are either 'in' or 'out' of prostitution, while little consideration is given to the changing levels and type of involvement that different women report.

Given the limited resources and evaluation skills available to most projects, some form of monitoring and evaluation, which is relatively easy to administer but robust and useful, needs to be developed. This evaluation needs to make allowances for reversals and lapses. In relation to outcomes, the number of women leaving prostitution is a significant measure, but alongside this we need to develop a series of 'soft' measures, such as the level of drug use, the level of involvement in prostitution, making contact with family and friends, organising accommodation, paying off debts, engaging in training and education, and the like.

Second, there are key issues around drug treatment and accommodation that need to be addressed. We have already made some comments on the need to develop more comprehensive and accessible forms of drug treatment not only for opiate users but also for those dependent on powder cocaine, crack cocaine, cannabis, amphetamines and alcohol. We have also suggested that there is an over-reliance on methadone and that, for a number of women at least, the aim should be abstinence rather than long-term dependency.

Providing accessible, manageable and affordable housing is a major challenge, and is clearly an important factor in relation to women's involvement in prostitution. We have suggested that the model developed by St Mungo's and Commonweal Housing provides an option that has proved to be effective. This model, however, needs to be developed and made more readily available across the country. At the same time other housing strategies need to be developed, to provide women with a place of safety and personal space in which they are able to reorganise their lives.

Debt remains a widespread barrier. Developing strategies that realistically allow women to deal with their financial problems is a necessity. Possibly a system of charity- or state-based loan schemes could be introduced in order to provide women with the funds to pay off existing debts and to reduce their dependence on the earnings they obtain from prostitution.

Dealing with the issue of criminalisation remains important. As our research has indicated that a significant number of women involved in prostitution have convictions for non-prostitution offences. In some cases these offences can be seen as a function of their drug dependency or their marginalised social position. There is an urgent need to reconsider the working of the Rehabilitation of Offenders Act (1974) in order to allow those with spent convictions for offences linked to prostitution to access legitimate employment.

The current position in relation to disclosure of criminal convictions is likely to have a fourfold effect on women involved in prostitution. First, the forms of employment and types of roles requiring enhanced disclosure are frequently the types that women exiting prostitution would like to access, such as working with other vulnerable people, working with children or in social care. Second, an offence under the Sexual Offences Act (1959) can never be 'filtered' under the existing process, and therefore many positions (paid or otherwise) that women exiting prostitution might apply for might lead to disclosure. Third, even if there is no conviction for soliciting or other listed offence, many women involved in prostitution are likely to have more than one offence, meaning that the new 'protected' status and 'filtering' of offences will have no direct benefit for these women. Fourth, the process of disclosure itself might reinforce stigma and interfere with women's attempts to break with the past, particularly if a woman repeatedly encounters this barrier when looking for work or as part of her attempts to re-engage with the social world through education, volunteering or when reconnecting with her family.

To resolve some of these issues, it is recommended that the Street Offences Act 1959 is removed from the list of recordable offences. Second, that the Street Offences Act (1959) be removed from the list of offences that can never be 'filtered'. While this will only benefit women who have had just one conviction for soliciting, this is still a step in the right direction. Third, in the event that the offence of soliciting under Section 1 of the Street Offences Act 1959 is removed as part of a wider shift in the legal settlement around prostitution, then it is recommended that historic records are 'deleted' in the same way that now legal homosexual acts have been treated under Section 92 of the Protection of Freedoms Act 2012. This will mean that if soliciting were decriminalised, women with a conviction for soliciting would be treated as if they had not been convicted of that offence.

A number of schemes have been designed to divert women offenders away from the criminal justice system (Rice 2010). Usually such schemes require women to participate to varying degrees with a support service, and usually to undertake some form of need assessment. While engagement with support is not usually a requirement, there is often some expectation that women remain involved with services for their own benefit. Schemes such as these have been evaluated, and while they offer some women clear benefits through keeping them out of the courts and preventing their prosecution, there have been a number of criticisms of such approaches (Easton et al. 2010). First, such schemes create the possibility of net-widening, where women who would otherwise be simply cautioned informally by the police end up with a formal caution on their record. While trying to reduce the number of women with convictions, this approach might have the unintended consequence of increasing the number of women who are given formal cautions. There is also concern that women who agree to a diversion in order to avoid court but fail to attend a support service might end up with harsher treatment in future than those who did not agree to the diversion in the first place.

There also remain some uncertainties about how to respond to and deal with 'partners' who may be living off the earnings of prostitution, or exercising some form of control over the women. In some areas such as Tower Hamlets in London and Ipswich, efforts have been made to either deal with women's involvement in prostitution in terms of domestic violence or by attempting alternatively to extricate the women from the grip of these 'partners'. More attention needs to be paid to this issue, since in some cases there is a personal relationship that has been established and one that the woman herself may be reluctant to terminate.

Conclusion and discussion

We have made a case for developing exiting strategies and for helping women involved in prostitution to make a positive change into a less exploitative and abusive lifestyle. We have suggested that such an approach is defensible on both humanistic and economic grounds. As an intervention or strategy we would suggest that we need to move beyond seeing women involved in prostitution as either wilful offenders or passive victims and see them as active agents, who in most cases require targeted and individualised support if they are to leave prostitution. These barriers will be different for those involved in on-street and off-street prostitution and those who have been trafficked.

We would argue that any responsible policymaker or politician who is seriously interested in addressing this issue needs to provide the necessary resources for making exiting programmes more widely available. The potential reduction of prostitution by the promotion of exiting programmes has considerable benefits not only for the women involved and their families and children but also for the wider community. However, despite what a growing number of commentators see as the undeniable benefits of exiting programmes, there remain a number of sceptics who continue to express doubts about the benefits of such strategies. These concerns need to be addressed.

In an article by Cusick et al. (2011), the authors question recent government policy on exiting, and since their concerns may be shared by others involved in this issue they require a response. They claim that:

- Exiting is a complex and lengthy process
- That problematic drug use is prevalent amongst women involved in prostitution and serves as a major barrier to exiting
- That current government policy on exiting is unlikely to meet its aims
- That the focus on exiting is likely to endanger or erode other aspects of support
- That the services associated with 'harm reduction' cannot be differentiated from those providing 'exiting' services
- Exiting projects do not address structural causes of prostitution
- Exiting programmes have no way of preventing new 'sex workers' replacing those who exit.

In response to these critiques of exiting it has been argued, first, that for many women exiting is not a complex and lengthy process. In fact, a major finding of our research and other related investigations is that many women are able to leave prostitution with a moderate degree of formal support, while some can be described as 'self-exiters'. Thus, while there often lapses and relapses many women are able to exit in a reasonable period of time.

Second, we have shown that there is a tendency in relation to this issue to overemphasise the role of drugs. Drug use and dependency was found in our study to be only one of a number of barriers to exiting, and that 'stabilising' women on substitute medications did not in itself always provide the main route out of prostitution. We have also made the point that effective interventions need to go beyond purely instrumental approaches and incorporate existential and emotional considerations, in the form of rebuilding trust and fostering hope with the aim of moving towards a more fulfilling life. Also, drug use is not the main or only factor associated with entry into prostitution, while we have seen that levels of drug use often increase as a result of involvement in prostitution. Moreover, the claim that women involved in off-street prostitution are not involved in regular and 'problematic' drug use is not the case, although their drugs of choice may be different from those involved in street prostitution.

Third, there are signs in recent years that the interest in exiting has decreased. This is not because of the difficulties implementing effective exiting programmes but a consequence of a change of political priorities and a lack of resources. As the examples of Ipswich and Glasgow indicate, where there is a clear political commitment to developing exiting strategies they can be extremely effective.

Fourth, the claim that developing exiting strategies is likely to erode other aspects of support is disingenuous. Rather, it is the case that many of the existing forms of support operate essentially to sustain women in prostitution rather than encouraging them to move on. Also, we have shown that exiting strategies involve a certain 'diffusion of benefits', providing long-term savings as well as freeing up other resources.

Fifth, the claim that the services provided by reactive harm reduction services are essentially the same as the proactive services provided by specialist exiting agencies is misconceived. We have developed a model above which combines the ability to address women's needs and build up trust and support on one hand with a proactive exiting strategy on the other, which is designed not to perpetuate the involvement of women in prostitution but rather to facilitate their exit.

Sixth, it is argued that women enter prostitution because of unemployment, poverty and debt, particularly in periods of economic crisis. However, much of the research on entry into prostitution points out that a considerable percentage of women and girls become involved in prostitution when they are children and are not part of the formal labour market (Matthews 2008). While it is the case that many women who enter prostitution are drawn from the poor and disadvantaged sections of society, poverty is a necessary but not sufficient explanation for their involvement.

Finally, the objection that exiting programmes do not prevent the recruitment of new women into prostitution is a spurious argument. Clearly, exiting strategies are not designed to prevent the future entry of women into prostitution any more than current desistance strategies are designed to prevent the emergence of new offenders. It is instructive to note that in both Ipswich and Glasgow the exiting programmes were accompanied by effective preventative projects.

In sum, we would suggest that the concerns expressed by Cusick et al. (2011) are misplaced and misconceived, and that exiting remains a viable and potentially extremely effective strategy for addressing the harms associated with prostitution, while allowing those caught up in the sex trade to exercise a degree of self-determination. Such strategies, if they are effective, will of course need to be properly funded and coordinated, and form part of a programme that is designed to reduce or remove the exploitative, coercive and abusive aspects of the sex trade.

References

Agranoff, R. (1977) 'Services Integration' in W. Anderson, B. Frieden and M. Murphy (eds.) *Managing Human Services*. Washington, DC: International City Management Association.

Anti-Trafficking Monitoring Group (2010) Wrong Kind of Victim? Anti Slavery International, http://www.antislavery.org/includes/documents/cm_docs/2010/f/full_report.pdf.

Archer, M. (1995) *Realist Social Theory: The Morphogenetic Approach*; Cambridge University Press.

Association of Chief Police Officers (2011) *ACPO Strategy and Supporting Operational Guidance for Policing Prostitution and Sexual Exploitation*. London: ACPO.

Audet, E. and Carrier, M. (2006) 'Green Light for Pimps and Johns'. *Sisyphe*. (http://www.sisyphe.org).

Austin, C. D. and McClelland, R. W. (2000) 'Case Management in Contemporary Human Services'. *Australian Journal of Case Management*, Vol.2, No.1: 4–8.

Baker, L., Dalla, R. and Williamson, C. (2010) 'Exiting Prostitution: An Integrated Model'. *Violence Against Women*, Vol.16, No.5: 579–600.

Beckett, K. and Herbert, S. (2008) 'Dealing with Disorder: Social Control in the Post- Industrial City' *Theoretical Criminology*, Vol.12, No.1: 5–30.

Ballew, J. R. and Mink, G. (1996) *Case Management in Social Work: Developing the Professional Skills Needed for Work with Multiproblem Clients*. Springfield, IL: Thomas.

Benoit, C. and Millar, A. (2001) *Dispelling the Myths and Understanding Realities: Working Conditions, Health Status, and Exiting Experiences of Sex Workers*. Victoria, BC: Canada Prostitutes Empowerment Education and Resource Society.

Bindel, J. (2006) *No Escape? An Investigation into London's Service Provision for Women Involved in the Commercial Sex Industry*. Poppy Project. London: Eaves Housing.

Bourgois, P. (2003) 'Crack and the Political Economy of Suffering'. *Addiction Research and Theory*, Vol.11, No.1: 31–37.

Boyer, D. (1989) 'Male Prostitution and Homosexual Identity' *Jornal of Homosexuality*, Vol.17, Nos. 1–2: 154–184.

Bourgois, P. and Schonberg, J. (2009) *Righteous Dopefiend*: University of California Press.

Boynton, P. (1998) *Somebody's Daughter, Somebody's Sister: A Reflection on Wolverhampton Working Women's Lives*. Wolverhampton: Ashton Business School.

Bradford, M. (2005) *Developing Exit Strategies for Female Outdoor Sex Workers in Barnet Enfield and Haringey*. London. Sexual Health Call.

Brewis, J. and Linstead, S. (2000) 'The Worst Thing is the Screwing: Consumption and the Management of Identity in Sex Work' *Gender, Work and Organisation*, Vol.7, No.2: 84–97.

Brown, A. and Barratt, D. (2002) *Child Prostitution and Child Sexual Abuse in Twentieth Century England*. Cullompton: Willan.

Browne, J., & Minichiello, V. (1995). The Social Meanings Behind Male Sex Work: Implications for Sexual Interactions'. *British Journal of Sociology*, Vol.32, No.1: 86–92.

Buchanan, J. (2004) 'Missing Links? Problem Drug Use and Social Exclusion'. *Journal of Community and Criminal Justice*, Vol.5, No.4: 387–399.

Burnett, R. and Maruna, S. (2004) 'So Prison Works, Does it?'. *Howard Journal of Criminal Justice*, Vol.43, No.4: 390–404.

Byford, S., Barrett, B., Metrebian, N., Groshkova, T., Cary, M., Charles, V. and Strang, J. (2013) 'Cost-effectiveness of Injectable Opioid Treatment v. Oral Methadone for Chronic Heroin Addiction'. *The British Journal of Psychiatry*, Vol.203, No.5: 341–349.

Carlsson, C. (2012) 'Using "Turning Points" to Understand Processes of Change in Offending'. *British Journal of Criminology*, Vol.52: 1–16.

Case Management Society of Australia (2004) *National Standards of Practice for Case Management*. Melbourne: Case Management Society of Australia.

Castillo, D., Gomoez, R., and Delgado, B. (1999) 'Border Lives: Prostitute Women in Tijuana' *Signs*, Vol.24: 387–422.

Cave, J., Hunt, P., Ismail, S., Levitt, R. Liccardo, R., Rabinovich, L., Rubin, J., and Weed, K. (2009 *Tackling Problem Drug Use*. RAND. National Audit office.

Christian, J., Veysey, B., Herrschaft, B. and Tubman-Carbone, H. (2009) 'Moments of Transformation: Formerly Incarcerated Individuals' Narratives of Change' in B. Veysey, J. Christian, and D. J. Martinez (eds.) *How Offenders Transform Their Lives*. Collumpton: Willan.

Church, S., Henderson, M., Barnard, M. and Hart, K. (2001) 'Violence by Clients Towards Female Prostitutes in Different Work Settings' *British Medical Journal* 332: 524–525.

Clarke, M. and Squires, S. (2005) 'Worlds Forever Apart? Using Vulnerable Adult Protection Policies to Deliver Better Health and Social Services to Street Prostitutes'. *Journal of Adult Protection*, Vol.7, No.1: 24–31.

Classen, C., Gronskaya, O. and Aggarwal, R. (2005) 'Sexual Revictimization: A Review of the Empirical Literature'. *Trauma, Violence Abuse*, Vol.6, No.2: 103–129.

Colley, H. (2003) 'Engagement Mentoring for Socially Excluded Youth: Problematising an "Holistic" Approach to Creating Employability Through the Transformation of Habitus'. *British Journal of Guidance and Counselling*, Vol.31, No.1: 77–99.

Corston, B. (2007) *A Review of Women with Particular Vulnerabilities in the Criminal Justice System*. London: Home Office.

Crawford, A. (1998) *Crime Prevention and Community Safety: Politics, Policies and Practices*. Harlow: Longman.

Cusick, L., Brooks-Gordon, B., Campbell, R. and Edgar, F. (2011) 'Exiting Drug Use and Sex Work: Career Paths, Interventions and Government Strategy Targets'. *Drugs Education Prevention and Policy*, Vol.18, No.12: 145–156.

Cusick, L. and Hickman, H. (2005) ' "Trapping" in Drug Use and Sex Work Careers' Drugs'. *Education Prevention and Policy*, Vol.12, No.5: 369–379.

Cusick, L., Martin, A. and May, T. (2003) *Vulnerability and Involvement in Drug Use and Sex Work*. Home Office Research Study 268. London: Home Office.

Cutajar, M., Ogloff, J., and Mullen, P. (2011) *Child Sexual Abuse and Subsequent Offending and Victimisation: A 45-Year Follow-Up Study*. Criminology Research Council.

Dalla, R. (2006) 'You Can't Hustle All Your Life: An Exploratory Investigation of the Exit Process amongst Street Level Prostituted Women'. *Psychology of Women Quarterly*, Vol.30: 276–290.

Day, S. (2007) *On the Game*. London: Pluto Press.

DePrince, A., Brown, L., cheit, R., Freyd, J., Gold, S., Pezdek, K. and Quinn, K. (2012) in R. Belli (ed.) *True and False Recovered Memories: Towards a Reconciliation of the Debate*: Springer.

Doran, C. M. (2008) 'Economic Evaluation of Interventions to Treat Opiate Dependence'. *Pharmacoeconomics*, Vol.26, No.5: 371–393.

Easton, H. (2007) *An Evaluation of the Prolific and Priority Offender Scheme in Four London Boroughs*. London: Government Office for London.

Easton, H., Silvestri, M., Evans, K., Matthews, R. and Walklate, S. (2010) *Conditional Cautions: Evaluation of the Women Specific Condition Pilot*. Ministry of Justice Research Series 14/10. London: Ministry of Justice.

Drugscope (2012) *The Challenge of Change: Improving Services for Women Involved in Prostitution and Substance Use*. London: The Pilgrim Trust.

Easton, H. and Matthews, R. (2008) *Vulnerable People with Chaotic Lifestyles*. London: London Borough of Greenwich.

Easton, H. and Matthews, R. (2012) *An Evaluation of the Chrysalis Project for Women Exiting Street Prostitution in Lambeth*. London: Commonweal Housing.

Ebaugh, H. (1988) *Becoming an Ex*. Chicago: Chicago University Press.

Epstein, M. and Bottoms, B. (2002) 'Explaining the Forgetting and Recovery of Abuse and Trauma Memories: Possible Mechanisms' *Child Maltreatment*, Vol.7: 210–225.

EMCDDA (2008) PDU Drug Use Population, Methods and Definitions, Statistical Bulletin, http://www.emcdda.europa.eu/stats08/pdu/methods.

Eustace, A. and Clarke, A. (2005) *Care and Case Management: Assessment of the Homeless Agency's Model*. Ireland: Homeless Agency.

Evashwick, C. (1997) *Seamless Connections: Refocusing Your Organization to Create a Successful Continuum of Care*. Chicago: American Hospital Publications.

Farley, M. (2003) *Prostitution Trafficking and Traumatic Stress*. New York: The Howarth Press.

Farley, M. (2004) 'Bad for the Body, Bad for the Heart; Prostitution Harms Women Even if it's Legalised or Decriminalised'. *Violence Against Women*, Vol.10, No.10: 1087–1125.

Farley, M. and Barkan, H. (1998) 'Prostitution, Violence and Stress Disorder', *Women and Health*, Vol.27, No.3: 37–49.

Farrall, S. and Bowling, B. (1999) 'Structuration, Human Development and Desistance from Crime'. *British Journal of Criminology*, Vol.39: 253–268.

Farrall, S. and Calverly, A. (2006) *Understanding Desistance from Crime*. Milton Keynes: Open University Press.

Flowers, R. (2001) *Runaway Kids and Teenage Prostitution*. Westport Connecticut: Praeger.

Frank, A. and Gunderson, J. G. (1990) 'The Role of the Therapeutic Alliance in the Treatment of Schizophrenia'. *Archives of General Psychiatry*, Vol.47: 228–236.

Giddens, A. (1979) *Central Problems in Social Theory: Action, Structure and Contradiction in Social Analysis*. University of California Press.

Gillies, P., Bolam, B., Johnson, S. and MacDonald, M. (2004) *A Cross Sectional Qualitative Study of the Impact of the Prostitute Outreach Workers Project in 2004*. Nottingham: Nottingham University.

Giordano, P., Cernkovich, S. and Rudolph, J. (2002) 'Gender, Crime and Desistance: Toward a Theory of Cognitive Transformation'. *American Journal of Sociology*, Vol.107, No.4: 990–1064.

Goffman, E. (2009) *Relations in Public*. New Brunswick: Transaction Publishers.

Goldstein, P. (1979) *Prostitution and Drugs*. Lexington, MA: Lexington Books.

Gossop, M., Manning, V., & Ridge, G. (2006) Concurrent Use of Alcohol and Cocaine: Differences in Patterns of Use and Problems Among Users of Crack Cocaine and Cocaine Powder. *Alcohol and Alcoholism*, Vol.41, No.2: 121–125.

Gossop, M., Marsden, J., Stewart, D. and Treacy, S. (2001) 'Outcomes after Methadone Maintenance and Methadone Reduction Treatments: Two-year Follow-up Results from the National Treatment Outcome Research Study'. *Drug and Alcohol Dependence*, Vol.62, No.3: 255–264.

Graham, J. and Bowling, B. (1995) *Young People and Crime*. Home Office Research Study No.145. London: Home Office.

Gronda, H. (2009) *What Makes Case Management Work for People Experiencing Homelessness? Evidence for Practice*. AHURI Final Report No. 127. Melbourne: Australian Housing and Urban Research Institute.

Haggarty, K. and Ericson, R. (2000) 'The Surveillant Assemblage'. *British Journal of Sociology*, Vol.51, No.4: 605–622.

Harcourt, C., Egger, S. and Donovan, B. (2005) 'Sex Work and the Law'. *Sexual Health*, Vol.2, No.3: 121–128.

Hedin, U.-C. and Mansson, S.-V. (2003) 'The Importance of Supportive Relationships Among Women Leaving Prostitution' in M. Farley (ed.) *Prostitution, Trafficking and Traumatic Stress*. New York: Haworth Press.

Heidensohn, F. (2006) *Gender and Justice: New Concepts and Approaches*. Cullompton: Willan.

Hepworth, D.H. and Larsen, J. (1982) *Direct Social Work Practice: Theory and Skills* Homewood, Illinois: Dorsey

Herman, J. (1992) *Trauma and Recovery*. New York: Basic Books.

Herman, J. (2003) 'Hidden in Plain Sight: Clinical Observations on Prostitution' in M. Farley (ed.) *Prostitution, Trafficking and Traumatic Stress.* Binghamton, NY: Haworth Press.

Hester, M. and Westmarland, N. (2004) *Tackling Street Prostitution: Towards a Holistic Approach.* Home Office Research Study 279. London: Home Office.

Hoigard, C. and Finstad, L. (1992) *Backstreets: Prostitution, Money and Love.* Cambridge: Polity Press.

Holmes, L., Westlake, D. and Ward, H. (2009) *Calculating and Comparing the Costs Of Multidimensional Treatment Foster Care, England (MTFCE),* Centre for Child and Family Research: Loughborough University.

Home Office (2004) *Paying the Price: A Consultation Paper on Prostitution.* London: Home Office.

Home Office (2006) *A Coordinated Prostitution Strategy and a Summary of Responses to Paying the Price.* London: Home Office.

Home Office (2013) *An Overview of Sexual Offending in England and Wales.* London: Home Office.

Hough, J. and Rice, B. (2008) *A Review of Services for Street- Based Women in Lambeth.* Broadway: London Borough of Lambeth.

Hubbard, P. (2004) 'Cleansing the Metropolis: Sex work and the Politics of Zero Tolerance' *Urban Studies,* Vol.41, No.9: 1687–1702.

Hunter, R. and Cowan, S. (2007) *Choice and Consent: Feminist Engagement with Law and Subjectivity,* London: Routledge.

Hubbard, P. (2006) 'Out of Touch and Out of Time? The Contemporary Policing of Sex Work' in R. Campbell and M. O'Neill (eds.) *Sex Work Now.* Cullompton: Willan.

Irving, A. and Laing, M. (2013) *PEER: Exploring the Lives of Sex Workers in Tyne and Wear.* Project Report. The Cyrenians, Newcastle-upon-Tyne.

Jackson, K., Jeffrey, J., and Adamson, G. (2010) *Setting the Record: The Trafficking of Migrant Women in the England and Wales Off-Street Prostitution Sector.* Project Acumen. ACPO.

James, J. (1976) Prostitution and addiction: An interdisciplinary approach. *Addictive Diseases: An International Journal,* 2(4), 601–618.

Jeal, N. and Salisbury, C. (2007) 'Health Needs and Service Use of Parlour-Based Prostitutes Compared with Street-Based Prostitutes', *BJOG, An International Journal of Obstetrics and Gyanecology,* Vol.114, No.7: 875–881.

Jeffreys, S. (1997) *The Idea of Prostitution.* Australia: Spinifex Press.

Kalant, H. (2010) 'Drug Classification: Science, Politics, Both or Neither?'. *Addiction,* Vol.105, No.7: 1146–1149.

Kantola, J. and Squires, J. (2004) 'Discourses Surrounding Prostitution Policies in the UK' *Women's Studies,* Vol.11: 77–101.

Kanzemain, L. (2007) 'Desistance from Crime: Theoretical, Empirical, Methodological and Policy Considerations'. *Journal of Contemporary Criminal Justice,* Vol.23, No.1: 5–27.

Katz, R. (2000) 'Explaining Girls and Women's Crime and Deviance in the Context of their Victimisation Experiences'. *Violence Against Women*, Vol.6, No.6: 633–660.

Kelly, L. (2003) 'The Wrong Debate: Reflections in Why Force is Not the Key Issue with Respect to Trafficking in Women for Sexual Exploitation', *Feminist Review*, Vol 73: 139–144.

Kinnel, H. (2006) 'Murder Made Easy: The Final Solution to Prostitution' In R. Campbell and M. O'Neill (eds.) *Sex Work Now*. Cullompton: Willan.

Kitzinger, C. (1996) 'Therapy and How it Undermines the Practice of Radical Feminism' in D. Klein and D. Bell (eds.) *Radically Speaking: Feminism Reclaimed*. Melbourne: Spinifex.

Laub, J. and Sampson, R. (2006) 'Turning Points in the Life Course: Why Change Matters to the Study of Crime'. *Criminology*, Vol.31, No.3: 301–325.

Lawrence, K. (2007) *Prostitution Strategy for Leeds*. Leeds: Safer Leeds Partnership.

LeBel, T. (2009) 'Formerly Incarcerated Persons Use of Advocacy/Activism as a Coping Orientation in the Reintegration Process' in B. Veysey, J. Christian and D. Martinez (eds.) *How Offenders Transform Their Lives*. Cullompton: Willan.

LeBel, T., Burnett, R., Maruna., and Bushway, S. (2008) 'The Chicken and Egg of Subjective and Social Factors in Desistance from Crime' *European Journal of Criminology*, Vol.5, No.2: 131–159.

Levesque, D., Prochaska, J. M. and Prochaska, J. O. (1999) 'Stages of Change and Integrated Service Delivery'. *Consulting Psychology Journal: Practice and Research*, Vol.51, No.4: 226–341.

Levine, I. S. and Fleming, M. (1985) Human Resource Development: Issues in Case Management. National Institute of Mental Health.

Levy, A. (2004) 'Stigmatised, marginalised and criminalised: An overview of the issues relating to children and young people involved in prostitution', London: NSPCC.

Lewis, K. and Montague, M. (2008) *Evaluation of Project Respect's Pathways Project. Project Respect.* Melbourne, Australia.

Littell, J. and Girvin, H. (2002) 'Stages of Change: A Critique'. *Behaviour Modification*, Vol.26: 223–273.

Manchester Prostitution Forum (2007) *Manchester Prostitution Strategy 2007–8*, http://www.manchester.gov.uk/egov_downloads/Appendix_1_Manchester_Strategy_2007.pdf.

Mansson, S.-V. and Hedin, U.-C. (1999) 'Breaking the Mathew Effect – On Women Leaving prostitution'. *British Journal of Social Welfare*, Vol.8: 67–77.

Maruna, S. (2001) *Making Good: How Ex-Convicts Reform and Rebuild Their Lives.* Washington, DC: American Psychologist Association.

Maruna, S., Immarigeon, R. and LeBel, T. (2004) 'Ex-Offender reintegration: Theory and Practice' in S. Maruna and R. Immarigeon (eds.) *After Crime and Punishment: Pathways to Offender Reintegration*. Cullompton: Willan.

Matthews, R. (2005) 'Policing Prostitution: Ten Years On' *British Journal of Criminology*, Vol.45: 1–20.

Matthews, R. (2008) *Prostitution, Politics and Policy*. London: Routledge.

Matthews, R., Easton., Briggs., and Pease, K. (2007) *Assessing Anti-Social Behaviour Orders*. Bristol: Policy Press.

Matthews, R. and Easton, H. (2010) *Prostitution and Glasgow: A Strategic Review*. Glasgow Community Safety Services. www.saferglasgow.com.

May, T. and Hunter, G. (2006) 'Sex Work and Problem Drug Use in the UK: The Links, Problems and Possible Solutions' in R. Campbell and M. O'Neill (eds.) *Sex Work Now*. Cullompton: Willan.

Mayhew, P. and Mossman, E. (2007) *Exiting Prostitution: Models of Best Practice*. New Zealand: Ministry of Justice.

McDonald, C. & Coventry, L. (2009) 'The Uses and Abuses of Case Management: A Critical Analysis of Contemporary Practices', in Moore, E. (2009) *Case Management for Community Practice South Melbourne, Victoria*: Oxford University Press.

McIvor, G., Murray, C. and Jamieson, J. (2004) 'Desistance from Crime: Is it Different for Women and Girls' in S. Maruna and R. Immarigeon (eds.) *After Crime and Punishment*. Cullompton: Willan.

McKeganey, N. (2005) 'Street Prostitution in Scotland: The View of Working Women' *Drugs, Education Prevention and Policy*, Vol.13, No.2: 151–166.

McNaughton, C. and Sanders, T. (2007) 'Housing and Transitional Phases out of "Disordered" Lives: The Case of Leaving Homelessness and Street Sex Work'. *Housing Studies*, Vol.22, No.6: 885–900.

McNeil, F. (2009) *Towards an Effective Practice of Offender Supervision* Report 01/09. Scottish Centre for Crime and Justice Research.

McNeill, F. and Weaver, B. (2010) *Changing Lives? Desistance Research and Offender Management*. Scottish Centre for Crime and Justice Research. Glasgow: University of Glasgow and Strathclyde.

Mead, S. & Copeland, M. E. (2000) What Recovery Means to Us: Consumers' Perspectives. *Community Mental Health Journal*, Vol.36, No.3: 315–328.

Melrose, M. (2007) 'The Governments New Prostitution Strategy: A Cheap Fix for Drug Using Sex Workers?'. *Community Safety Journal*, Vol.6, No.1: 18–27.

Melrose, M., Barrett, D. and Brodie, I. (1999) *One Way Street?: Retrospectives on Child Prostitution*. London: The Children's Society.

Messerschmidt, J. (1993) *Masculinities and Crime: Critique and Reconcep- tuatlization of Theory*. Maryland: Rowan & Littlefield Publishers, Inc.

Miller, P. (2001) 'A Critical Review of the Harm Minimisation Ideology in Australia'. *Critical Public Health*, Vol.11, No.2: 167–178.

Misztal, B. (1996) *Trust in Modern Societies*. Cambridge: Polity Press.

Moxley, D. P. (1989) *The Practice of Case Management*. London: Sage.

Ng, J. and Venticich, M. (2006) *Another Route: Pathways for Women in the Sex Industry*. Melbourne, Australia: Project Respect.

Nutt, D. J., King, L. A. and Phillips, L. D. (2010) 'Drug Harms in the UK: A Multicriteria Decision Analysis'. *The Lancet*, Vol.376, No.9752: 1558–1565.

O'Neill, M. (2001) *Prostitution and Feminism: Towards a Politics of Feeling*. Cambridge: Polity.

O'Neill, M. and Campbell, R. (2011) 'Desistance from Sex Work: Feminist Cultural Criminology and Intersectionality: The Complexities of Moving in and Out of Sex Work' in Y. Taylor, S. Hines and M. Casey (eds.) *Theorizing Intersectionality and Sexuality*. Basingstoke: Palgrave Macmillan.

Oselin, S. (2009) 'Leaving the Streets: Transformation of Prostitute Identity within the Prostitution Rehabilitation Programme'. *Deviant Behavior*, Vol.30: 379–406.

PAAFE (2005) *Breaking Down Barriers: One Step at a Time*. Prostitution Awareness and Action Foundation. Canada: Edmonton. (http://www.paafe.org).

Partridge, S. (2004) *Examining Case Management Models of Community Sentences*. Home Office Online Report 17/04. London: Home Office.

Pawson, R. and Tilley, N. (1997) *Realistic Evaluation*. London: Sage.

Pitcher, J. (2006) 'Support Services for Women Working in the Sex Industry' in R. Campbell and M. O'Neill (eds.) *Sex Work Now*. Cullompton: Willan.

Poland, F., Boswell, G. and Killet, A. (2008) *Evaluation Research Report Ipswich Street Prostitution Strategy 2007–8*. University of East Anglia.

Poland, F., Boswell, G. and Killet, A. Jarrett, J., Fordham, R. Houghton, J., Varley, A. and Seebohm, L. (2012) *Evaluation Research Report for Ipswich/Suffolk Prostitution Strategy 2007–2012*: Evissta 2, University of East Anglia.

Potterat, J., Rothenberg, R., Muth, S., Darrow, W. and Phillips-Plummer, L. (1998) 'Pathways to Prostitution: The Chronology of Sexual and Drug Abuse Milestones'. *Journal of Sex Research*, Vol.35, No.4: 333–340.

Prochaska, J., DiClemente, C. and Norcross, J. C. (1992) 'In Search of How People Change'. *American Psychologist*, Vol.49, No.9: 1102–1114.

Radcliffe, P., Hunter, G. and Vass, R. (2013) *The Development and Impact of Community Services for Women Offenders: An Evaluation*. London: ICPR.

Raphael, J. and Shapiro, D. (2004) 'Violence in Indoor and Outdoor Venues' *Violence Against Women*, Vol.10, No.2: 126–139.

Rapp, C. A. (1998) The Active Ingredients of Effective Case Management. *Community Mental Health Journal*, Vol 34, No.4: 363–380.

Raymond, J. (2013) *Not a Choice, Not a Job*. Washington: Potomac Books.

Rayner, K. (2006) 'Homelessness and Drug Addiction: Model Overview and Outcomes of the Homeless and Drug Dependency Trial's Multi-faceted Approach to Assisting those with Complex Health and Social Needs'. *Just Policy*, Vol.40: 35–42.

Research Synthesis. *Community Mental Health Journal*, Vol.34, No.4: 363–380.

Rice, B. (2010) *Independent Evaluation of the Safe Exit Diversion Scheme*. Toynbee Hall, London: Accendo.

Riley, D., Sawka, E., Conley, P., Hewitt, D., Mitic, W., and Poulin, C. (1999) 'Harm Reduction: Concepts and Practice'. A Policy Discussion Paper. *Substance Use & Misuse*, Vol.34: 9–24.

Roe, G. (2005) 'Harm Reduction as a Paradigm: Is Better than Bad Good Enough?'. *Critical Public Health*, Vol.15, No.3: 243–250.

Rose, S. R. (1992) *Case Management and Social Work Practice*. White Plains, NY: Longman.

Ross, H. (1980) *Proceedings of the Conference on the Evaluation of Case Management Programs*, Los Angeles: Volunteers for Service to Older Persons.

Ross, C., Farley, M., and Schwartz, H. (2003) 'Dissociation Among Women in Prostitution' in M. Farley (ed.) *Prostitution, Trafficking and Traumatic Stress*. New York: Haworth Press.

Rothman, J. (1992) *Guidelines for Case Management: Putting Research to Professional Use*. Itasca, IL.: F.E. Peacock Publishers.

Rumgay, J. (2004) 'Scripts for Safer Survival: Pathways Out of Female Crime'. *The Howard Journal*, Vol.43, No.4: 405–419.

Sagar, T. (2007) 'Tackling On-Street Sex Work: Anti-Social Behaviour Orders, Sex Workers and Inclusive Inter-Agency Initiatives' *Criminology and Criminal Justice*, Vol.7: 153–168.

Sampson, R. and Laub, J. (1993) *Crime in the Making: Pathways and Turning Points Through Life*. Cambridge, MA: Harvard University Press.

Sampson, R. and Laub, J. (2003) 'Desistance from Crime over the Life Course' in J. Mortimer and M. J. Shanahan (eds.) *Handbook of the Life Course*. New York: Kluwer.

Sanders, T. (2005) *Sex Work: A Risky Business*. Cullompton: Willan.

Sanders, T. (2007) 'Becoming an Ex-Sex Worker: Making Transitions Out of a Deviant Career'. *Feminist Criminology*, Vol.2, No.1: 74–95.

Sanders, T., and Campbell, R. (2007). Designing out Vulnerability, Building in Respect: Violence, Safety and Sex Work Policy. *The British Journal of Sociology*, Vol.58, No.1: 1–19.

Sandwith, L. (2011) *Score, Smoke. Back on the Beat: An Exploration of the Impact of Homelessness on Exiting Street Sex Working in Manchester*. The Griffiths Society.

Saphira, M. and Oliver, P. (2002) 'A Review of the Literature on Child Prostitution'. *Social Policy Journal of New Zealand*, Vol.19: 141–163.

Scottish Executive (2004) *Being Outside: Constructing a Response to Street Prostitution*. Edinburgh: Scottish Executive.

Smith, F. and Marshall, L. (2007) 'Barriers to Effective Drug Addiction Treatment for Women Involved in Street Level Prostitution' *Criminal Behaviour and Mental Health*, Vol.7: 163–170.

Silbert, H. and pines, A. (1982) 'Entrance into Prostitution' *Youth and Society*, Vol.13, No.4: 471–500.

Sommers, I., Baskin, D. and Fagan, J. (1994) 'Getting Out of the Life: Crime Desistance by Female Street Offenders'. *Deviant Behaviour*, Vol.15, No.2: 125–149.

Stephens, D., Dennis, E., Toomer, M. and Holloway, J. (1991) 'The Diversity of Case Management Needs for the Care of Homeless Persons'. *Public Health Reports*, Vol.106, No.1: 15–19.

Surratt, H. L., Inciardi, J. A., Kurtz, S. P., & Kiley, M. C. (2004). Sex Work and Drug Use in a Subculture of Violence. *Crime and Delinquency*, Vol.50: 43–59.

Sutton, K. (1996) 'Can Stages of Change Provide Guidance in the Treatment of Addcitions?' in G. Edwards and C. Pate (eds.) *Psychotherapy, Psychological Treatments and the Addictions*. Cambridge University Press.

Swift, T. (2005) *Routes out of Prostitution: Evaluation of the Intervention Team*. Glasgow Social Inclusion Partnership. Glasgow City Council.

UKNSWP (2008) *Working With Sex Workers: Exiting. Good Practice Guidance UK. Network of Sex Work Projects*. Manchester. (http://www.uknswp.org).

Upston, B. (1994) *Case Management and the Supported Accommodation Assistance Program: A Report to Health and Community Services Victoria*. Melbourne: Centre for Social Health.

Vanderplasschen, W., Rapp, R. C., Wolf, J. R. and Broekaert, E. (2004) 'The Development and Implementation of Case Management for Substance Use Disorders in North America and Europe'. *Psychiatric Services*, Vol.55, No.8: 913–922.

Vanwesenbeeck, I. (1994). *Prostitutes' Well-Being and Risk*. VU University Press.

Vanwesenbeeck, I. (2001) 'Another Decade of Social Scientific Work on Sex Work: A Review of Research 1990–2000' *Annual Review of Sex Research*, Vol.12: 242–275.

Vaughan, B. (2007) 'The Internal Narrative of Desistance'. *British Journal of Criminology*, Vol.47, No.3: 390–404.

Wacquant, L. (1990) 'Exiting Roles or Exiting Role Theory? Critical Notes'. *Ebaugh's Becoming an Ex. Acta Sociologica*, Vol.33, No.4: 399–404.

Wahab, S. (2005) 'Violence in the Sex Industry' *Journal of Interpersonal Violence*, Vol.20, No.3: 263–269.

Ward, K. (2007) *In Pieces: A Review of Prostitution, Community Safety Issues and Good Practice*. Report for Ipswich Voluntary Services.

Ward, T. and Brown, S. (2004) 'The Good Lives Model and Conceptual Issues in Offender Rehabilitation'. *Psychology, Crime and Law*, Vol.10: 243–257.

Ward, T. and Maruna, S. (2007) *Rehabilitation*. London: Routledge.

Warren, E., Viney, R., Shearer, J., Shanahan, M., Wodak, A. and Dolan, K. (2006) 'Value for Money in Drug Treatment: Economic Evaluation of Prison Methadone'. *Drug and Alcohol Dependence*, Vol.84, No.2: 160–166.

Weeks, M. Grier, M. Romero-Daza., N., Puglisi-Vasquez, M. Singer, M. (1998) Streets, drugs, and the economy of sex in the age of AIDS in Stevens, S., Tortu, S. and Coyle, S (eds) *Women, drug use and HIV infection*, New York: Haworth Medical Press.

Weitzer, R. (2005) 'New Directions in Research on Prostitution' *Crime, Law and Social Change*, Vol.43: 211–235.

Wolff, N., Helminiak, T. W., Morse, G. A., Calsyn, R. J., Klinkenberg, W. D. & Trusty, M. L. (1997) Cost-Effectiveness Evaluation of Three Approaches to

Case Management for Homeless Mentally Ill Clients. *American Journal of Psychiatry*, Vol.154: 341–348.

Young, A., Boyd, C. and Hubbell, A. (2000) 'Prostitution, drug use and coping with psychological distress', *Journal of Drug Issues*, Vol.30, No.4: 789–800.

Index

Printed and bound by CPI Group (UK) Ltd, Croydon, CR0 4YY